HEATH ROBINSON
ADVERTISING

Portrait of W. Heath Robinson aged 43, first published in *The Sketch* in November 1915.

HEATH ROBINSON ADVERTISING

Edited and Introduced by
Geoffrey Beare

BELLEW PUBLISHING
London

OTHER TITLES IN THE CARTOON LIBRARY
(General Editor: Mark Bryant)

The Complete Colonel Blimp edited by Mark Bryant
(Foreword by Rt Hon. Michael Foot, Introduction by Colin Seymour-Ure)

Gibbard's Double Decade Omnibus
edited and introduced by Les Gibbard
(Foreword by John Cole)

The Last Bohemian: G.L. Stampa of Punch
edited and introduced by Flavia Stampa Gruss
(Foreword by David Thomas)

JON'S Complete Two Types edited and introduced by JON
(Foreword by Lord Cudlipp)

For Geraldine

First published in Great Britain in 1992 by
Bellew Publishing Company Limited
7 Southampton Place, London WC1A 2DR

ISBN 1 857250 39 7

Printed and bound in Great Britain by SRP Ltd, Exeter
Typesetting by Goodfellow & Egan, Cambridge

PREFACE

THIS book, whose publication marks the 120th anniversary of the birth of William Heath Robinson (1872–1944), sets out to record and promote the one major area of that artist's output that has previously been inaccessible – the large number of his drawings and paintings commissioned for the purposes of advertising and publicity. This anniversary is also marked in London in 1992 by major exhibitions of his work at the Royal Festival Hall and at Chris Beetles Ltd. Little of Heath Robinson's advertising work has survived in its original form, and so tracking down his commercial output has been a slow and painstaking activity. The considerable assistance received in preparing the unique bibliography, published here for the first time, is acknowledged separately in that section of the book. However, I must also thank the staff of the National Newspaper Library at Colindale for their friendly cooperation during my long periods of research there, and also Mr R. W. Smallwood of GKN, Mr N. F. Shattock of United Distillers and Mr D. Dunkley of Rank, Hovis Ltd for providing information from their archives. Thanks too must go to Connolly Brothers, Chris Beetles Ltd, *Punch*, *Daily Mail* and *Illustrated London News* for providing source material for illustrations, and especially to the Trustees of the Estate of the Late J. C. Robinson without whose support this book would not have been possible.

Finally, I must express my gratitude to Bellew Publishing for taking on the project, to Richard Kelly for designing the book, and especially to Mark Bryant whose cheerful encouragement and professionalism have ensured that the final product is worthy of its subject.

G.C.B.

TESTING CONNOLLY
LEATHER FOR IT'S
REACTION TO ALL
ATMOSPHERIC CON-
DITIONS BY TAKING
COWS INTO THE STRATOSPHERE

(*Illustration from* Connolly-Land, 1934)

CONTENTS

An advertisement for Sandy Macdonald Scotch Whisky that was published in
The Sketch Christmas number, 1922.

INTRODUCTION

At the turn of the century only a minority of advertisements in periodicals were illustrated, and the majority of those that were included relatively prosaic drawings of the product being promoted. There were some notable exceptions such as Bovril's advertisement featuring a bull looking at a jar of their product and lamenting his poor brothers. Others included comic drawings of monkeys for Brooke's 'Monkey Brand' soap and Pears' use of the *Punch* cartoon by Harry Furniss 'I used your soap two years ago, since when I have used no other' to advertise their soap. However, these examples were intended to reassure the reader by their familiarity rather than impress him with their wit and originality, being used repeatedly over many years.

During the first two decades of the twentieth century a small number of companies, usually influenced by American connections, started to employ humorous artists regularly for advertising, and from about 1920 the use of humour in advertising became widespread, with most of the successful cartoonists of the day being thus employed. For many of them this work would have provided an important part of their income, such drawings generally commanding higher prices than equivalent magazine contributions, although with the proviso that advertising work was usually sold outright, whilst the artist retained both subsequent publication rights and the original artwork for contributions to magazines.

Heath Robinson first became involved in advertising in 1903, when the modern approach to the subject was in its infancy, and continued to work for a wide range of companies until shortly before his death in 1944. Much of his work was for trade periodicals or for promotional booklets to be distributed at trade exhibitions, and so had a limited circulation. Magazine advertisements were usually torn out and discarded before the single issues were bound into volumes, so few printed examples survive to the present. Also, few companies kept archives of past advertising material or took care to preserve the original artwork that they had commissioned once it had served its primary purpose. For these reasons the advertising work of humorous artists is often hard to find and has been relatively neglected. However, the high fees such work commanded, and the superior printing processes that were often employed, mean that the quality of both the ideas and finish of such drawings is frequently above average, and repays the efforts of the diligent collector.

Beginnings In Advertising

The third son of the wood-engraver and illustrator Thomas Robinson, William Heath Robinson was born in Islington in North London on 31 May 1872. His formal training as an artist began at Islington Art School and was continued at The Royal Academy Schools. On leaving art school Heath Robinson's first inclination was to landscape painting, which remained his first love throughout his life, but economic realities soon forced him to turn to a more readily saleable form of art. His older brothers, Charles and Tom, had already established themselves as book illustrators, and he joined them, starting in a small room off his father's studio. His first attempts to sell his work to London publishers met with little success, but eventually he managed to sell a number of drawings for publication in the *Sunday* magazine in 1896. From that time his career blossomed rapidly, and by 1900, when he illustrated *The Poems of Edgar Allan Poe* for George Bell, he had, according to *The Studio* magazine, established himself as a 'worthy disciple of the modern school of penmen'.

By 1903 Heath Robinson was getting a steady flow of book-work. His main patron at the time was Grant Richards, who had published the first book that he had both written and illustrated, a delightful children's story called *The Adventures of Uncle Lubin*. It was as a result of this book that his introduction to the world of advertising occurred in 1903, when he received a letter from an American, Chas Ed Potter. After reading *The Adventures of Uncle Lubin*, Potter had determined that its creator was the ideal artist to illustrate some advertisements that he had been writing for the Lamson Paragon Supply Company of Canning Town, London. The company's activities included the manufacture of check books, which enabled traders to keep detailed records of their transactions, 'Plic Books' (which would give a carbon duplicate from a pen-and-ink written original) and paper bags. Advertising drawings were required not only to promote these products in various trade journals, but also for use as 'stock blocks' for clients' advertisements on paper bags or on the backs of receipts.

View of Paragon Works, Canning Town, London, E. where Paragon productions are manufactured Thrice round means a mile.

The Lamson Paragon factory in Canning Town, London, when it was built in the 1890s, contained the most modern machinery for the printing and manufacture of check books, duplicate books and paper bags, as well as providing excellent facilities for staff. It was destroyed in the Blitz.

10

Heath Robinson's first advertising drawing, for Lamson Paragon Supply Co. Ltd, was published in *The Grocer* and other trade magazines on 25 April 1903.

Potter invited Heath Robinson to meet him in Tranter's Hotel, near St Paul's Cathedral, to discuss the project. Having heard many tales of American confidence tricksters coming to England and taking advantage of the unwary and innocent, Heath Robinson was suspicious, but agreed to make some drawings as long as he received payment in cash for each one when it was delivered. Every two or three days for the next few weeks he called at the hotel to deliver his drawings, for which he was paid in gold sovereigns, and to plan the next set. These transactions not only laid the basis of a friendship that endured throughout his life, but also provided the financial security that allowed him to marry. Writing to Potter in Canada a year later, he said that:

I am quite an old married man now it seems, at least I am quite used to this state, and took to it quite naturally. I had hoped to introduce you to my wife had you come over this time, but still we hope there may be an opportunity someday. She well remembers your visit to this country and the sudden access of wealth your being in London meant for us, and just at the right moment too.

The first of the drawings that Potter had commissioned from Heath Robinson for Lamson Paragon appeared in *The Grocer* on 25 April 1903. It showed a man about to cut off the ear of a shopkeeper, and headed a half-page advertisement for Paragon Check Books in which the copy began: 'Are you satisfied with your sales system? If you are, don't waste time reading further. We want the ear of the progressive shopkeeper – the one who is not satisfied.' Similar drawings were used in advertisements for Paragon Check Books for the next seven weeks, and the sequence was then repeated. This initial campaign must have been deemed a success, since a further eighteen drawings appeared in weekly Lamson Paragon advertisements in *The Grocer* later in 1903 and these were reused until April 1904.

Chas Ed Potter's stay in London was a short one, since by April 1903 he was in Toronto, where he was to continue his advertising activities for many years, working for the City Dairy Company and also acting as a freelance advertising agent. He commissioned further work from Heath Robinson, including a four-colour cover for a booklet issued by the City Dairy Company and a number of poster designs which he hoped to sell to local businesses.

Potter recommended as his successor at Lamson Paragon another American, John Meath Evans of Buffalo, N.Y. At the time Evans was running a small printing business, the White–Evans Penfold Company, with two partners. Evans arrived in England to take up his new post on a trial basis early in 1904, and one of his first actions was to contact Heath Robinson to invite him to make some more drawings for Lamson Paragon. On 18 March 1904 the artist wrote to Potter in Toronto:

For some little time I have been intending to write to you telling you that the Lamson Paragon Company have sent for me to do some drawings for them. Have I to thank you for giving them my address?

Heath Robinson and J.M. Evans got off to a good start. On arriving in England in March 1904, Evans was invited to work in Heath Robinson's studio in New Court, Carey St, off Chancery Lane, and in a letter to Potter in September that year Heath Robinson wrote: 'I got on very well indeed with Mr Evans and I am sure we worked well together. In fact my dealings with Americans have been a great pleasure to me.'

To J. M. Evans.
In memory of our friendly collaboration of many years ago
W. H. R.
1941.

Evans and Heath Robinson discussing ideas for Lamson Paragon advertisements, a sketch made for J.M. Evans by Heath Robinson on the half-title of a presentation copy of *My Line of Life*, the artist's autobiography, in 1941.

The weekly half-page advertisements for Paragon Check Books continued throughout 1904 in *The Grocer* and similar trade journals, and during 1905 the company started to take a full page, running two advertisements at a time. In the autumn of 1904 Evans had returned to America to sell out his share in the White-Evans Penfold company, and he then settled permanently in England. A closer working relationship now began to develop between artist and copy-writer. Heath Robinson would meet Evans once a week to hand over drawings and discuss ideas for the future. Following sound Lamson Paragon business principles, Evans would write the idea to be illustrated in a Plic book, giving Heath Robinson the top copy and retaining the duplicate. After discussion of how the subject might be treated, sometimes resulting in a rough sketch in Evans' book, Heath Robinson would set to work, delivering the finished drawing at the following week's meeting. Subjects were sometimes quotations from Shakespeare or other literary figures, but more often original ideas. Frequently used themes were: profits leaking away without the pro-prietor's knowledge, because he lacks the security provided by a check book system; the time wasted making manual copies or using a copying press – more efficient to use a Plic book; and the false economy of using inferior materials, e.g. cheap paper bags that spill customers' goods, thereby risking their goodwill to save a few pence.

During 1905–6 Heath Robinson made at least 90 drawings for Lamson Paragon, some of which were still being used, for example in company sales bulletins, as late as 1919. 'The Worried Man' is typical and was used to advertise both check books and Plic books. At the Grocery, Provision, Oil and Italian Warehouse and Allied Trades 13th Annual International Exhibition and Market, held in the Agricultural Hall in London from 16 to 23 September 1905, Lamson Paragon took two prominent positions on the ground floor. According to *The Grocer*:

The second stand was embellished with original drawings, which the company had prepared for advertising matter for the trade. This was a somewhat new departure, but the enterprise we fancy will be successful.

An accompanying photograph showed the second stand in the form of a shop front with large-scale drawings by Heath Robinson forming panels under the windows and other designs displayed in the windows.

Also during 1904–5 a number of Heath Robinson drawings were used to advertise Lamson Paragon's M & M Paragon typewriter ribbons and Paragon carbon paper. The *Stationery Trades Journal* in October 1904 reported that the company had erected a series of enamelled metal mural advertisements for their products at principal railway stations. Heath Robinson's design showed a telegraph boy with winged feet hurrying to bring a giant M & M Paragon typewriter ribbon, in its distinctive yellow box, to an attractive young typist seated at her machine, which was reproduced in blue and yellow.

The additional income derived from his advertising work must have been particularly welcome to Heath Robinson at this time. In 1904 Grant Richards had set him to work on his most ambitious project to date, a new edition of the

'The Worried Man', one of the few surviving drawings made by Heath Robinson for Lamson Paragon.

works of Rabelais in two lavishly produced volumes with over 200 drawings. Sadly, however, the costs involved in publishing such extravagant books had led to the publisher's bankruptcy, which was announced in November 1904. The creditors, of whom Heath Robinson was one, eventually received a dividend of only two shillings in the pound.

The loss of his main patron, together with any hope of payment for his recently completed work must have come as a blow, especially as he was now the father of a baby girl. He therefore started to look for new sources of income in addition to advertising and decided that his best prospect lay with the quality magazines, which paid well and gave a quick return. What they wanted were large, well-drawn comic pictures, and this is what he produced. In his first attempts in the new field he drew on the experience gained whilst working with Potter and Evans, producing comic illustrations to quotations from the classics,

TO WORRIED MEN

TO those who worry, it's useless saying "Don't" or reciting platitudes, such as, "It's not work but worry that kills," etc. What the worried man wants is a remedy—a remove-the-cause preventative.

Isn't that so, Worried Man ?

Well, here's our little lot of advice :

For worrying about your cash—or forgetting to charge—or disputes with customers, etc., etc.,—PARAGON CHECK BOOKS.

For worrying about what you wrote last week—whether or not you ordered some goods you badly need now—PARAGON PLIC BOOKS AND PLIC POST-CARD BOOKS.

Thousands are using the above remedies and have quit worrying. You can go on, if you wish, but our advice is : "Don't ; it doesn't pay and it ruins your health in the bargain."

Write to Dept. 3 for samples and prices, or if in town, call at our City Office and Salesroom, 4 St. Paul's Churchyard, E.C.

BIRMINGHAM OFFICE: 7A WARWICK PASSAGE

SOUTH AFRICA: 58 FLETCHER'S CHAMBERS DARLING STREET, CAPE TOWN

LAMSON PARAGON SUPPLY CO., L'T'D
Check Books, Plic Books, Paper Bags
CANNING TOWN, LONDON, E

OLIVER WANTS MORE

HE'S ASKING FOR MORE.

It's the old, old story.

It went on before Oliver Twist's time, and it's been going on ever since, and it will keep going on.

Is your assistant worth an increase ?

Look over his sales, and see how much more he's selling than he did last year, or than his junior assistant.

If you don't know this, you ought to.

You don't pass an invoice for payment until you've checked it and examined the goods, do you ? You want to know what you're getting for your money, don't you ?

And yet you pay your assistant without knowing what you get in return.

It's not fair to you or him, is it ?

Paragon Checks solve the difficulty.

It will only take a minute to write Dept. 1 for samples and prices, or if in town, call at our City Office, 4, Queen Street, E.C.

'To Worried Men', an advertisement in *The Grocer* in October 1906.

'Oliver Wants More', from *The Drapers' Record* in June 1905.

15

'My Annual Turnover', one of Heath Robinson's most attractive drawings for Lamson Paragon, was published in *The Drapers' Record* in January 1905.

but he found it difficult to get started. One editor looking at his early attempts commented 'If this work is humorous, your serious work must be very serious indeed.' However, in 1905 he sold a number of pictures to *The Bystander* and *The Tatler*, and in 1906 *The Sketch* published a series of cartoons called 'The Gentle Art of Catching Things' which established him as one of the leading comic artists of the day. The mechanical element first entered his work with the series 'Great British Industries – Duly Protected' in *The Sketch* in early 1909.

Heath Robinson's involvement with Lamson Paragon declined after 1908, when his book-work began to pick up again with a commission for 40 large watercolour illustrations to *Twelfth Night*. During the years from 1906 to 1916 he successfully combined the careers of comic artist and serious illustrator, producing what was to be his best work in both fields. This was the age of the gift book with its sumptuous binding and tipped-in coloured plates. His contributions to the genre included editions of Shakespeare's plays, Kipling's poetry, Hans Andersen's and Perrault's fairy tales and *Bill the Minder*, a children's story that he both wrote and illustrated. His black-and-white illustrations to *A Midsummer Night's Dream* rank amongst the finest produced for any book this century. It must have taken considerable discipline to create such books and at the same time to draw the outrageously absurd pictures that were appearing regularly in *The Bystander*, *The Sketch* and a number of other magazines. None the less, his connection with Lamson Paragon was maintained throughout the First World War and into the 1920s. A number of his cartoons, many of them on the theme 'safety first', appeared in *Paragon Way*, the company's house magazine in 1920–1.

Although somewhere between two and three hundred of his drawings for Lamson Paragon had appeared in various trade magazines from 1903 until

1909, by 1915 they were sufficiently forgotten that a journalist called Lampeter Todd writing in *Advertising World* about Heath Robinson's art could say that:

Up to the present Heath Robinson has not done much for advertising purposes; only a few drawings for Press announcements . . . and one or two posters, the latter, as he remarks, 'not at all characteristic'.

This despite the fact that four of Heath Robinson's drawings for Lamson Paragon were illustrated in the article. Apparently a Mr Hunt, an associate of Chas Ed Potter, wrote to *Advertising World* to protest at the failure to give greater prominence to this important and innovative body of work. The magazine did not publish the letter, but passed it on to Heath Robinson, who said in his reply in March 1916:

I do so little advertising work nowadays that is advertising in the same sense as my earlier work used to be, that I am afraid I did not give sufficient importance to this side of my work, or to its history in my interview with the writer of the article. I regret this now, if for no other reason that I have missed an opportunity of acknowledging the sympathetic collaboration of those with whom I worked, and certainly foremost amongst them was my good friend Mr Potter to whom I am greatly indebted for my introduction to the Lamson Paragon Company.

Despite its overlooking Heath Robinson's early commercial work, the article does contain a number of perceptive insights, stating that:

Heath Robinson's work is always arrestingly individual. He possesses a rare faculty for applying the most ancient and firmly-established principles of decorative art in a fresh and original manner . . .

He should be induced to do more for the advertiser; more especially, perhaps, as a humorous draughtsman, for here he brings to the service of those who use his work the value of a reputation that is practically world-wide, in addition to the intrinsic worth of his productions . . .

For myself, I should also particularly like to see some Heath Robinson posters on the hoardings, and by no means primarily works of a humorous character. The artist's fine sense of structural design, his exceptional skill in handling broad, flat masses, and the simple directness with which he expresses himself in line and tone all point to him as *in posse* a designer of posters of a distinction far beyond the ordinary.

Sadly, it is unlikely that more than half a dozen of the original drawings that Heath Robinson made for Lamson Paragon survive, since the company's Canning Town Works, where their printing was done, was destroyed by enemy bombing during the Second World War.

CARTOONS FOR COMMERCE

From the outbreak of the First World War the production of gift books was gradually stifled by increasing restrictions and the shortage of paper, and by the end of the war the market for such books had disappeared. Heath Robinson had therefore to depend entirely on the humorous side of his work for his income. His wartime cartoons had proved immensely popular with servicemen overseas and with his readers at home, and so he was greatly in demand with magazine editors. His mechanical inventions came into their own, first in showing 'German Breaches of the Hague Convention' such as the use of button magnets, then in his series of 'Inventions Rejected by the Invention Board'. These included the Pilsner-pump for stealing the enemy's supper beer, the Barb-drawer for extracting barbs from enemy wire and the Armoured Corn-crusher for treading on the enemy's toes. On the home front in 1915 he introduced his cartoon style to the world of advertising.

Heath Robinson's first major advertising project after Lamson Paragon was for R.J. Lea Ltd of Manchester, to advertise their 'Chairman' tobacco. This took the form of a series of twelve humorous pen-and-wash drawings illustrating the twelve virtues of 'Chairman'. Undoubtedly, Heath Robinson had a hand in selecting the virtues to be illustrated, for whilst some are those that would obviously occur to any advertising agent, others betray the artist's unique style of humour. The manufacturer himself would have insisted on promoting its attractive aroma, the entire absence of burning sensation, that it suits most palates, or that it is an economy. He would have been unlikely to have suggested that it is 'a solace to the very end' or insisted on promoting 'its taking qualities' and only Heath Robinson could have suggested that 'it promotes Mark Tapleyism'.

The drawings are in the style of his contemporary cartoons in *The Sketch* and other periodicals and, in both concept and execution, match the best of them. They also contain a wealth of amusing detail in addition to the main subject, often involving the already famous Heath Robinson birds, or other animals. In 'It's Attractive Aroma', the first of the series, an elderly man is sitting at an open window smoking 'Chairman' and reading his newspaper, while an airman lowers himself on a knotted string to steal a puff from the pipe. Above, a small bird is stretching its neck over the coping to inhale the rising smoke. The second, illustrating 'A solace to the very end' shows the pipe-smoker disappearing down the throat of a crocodile, a contented smile on his face.

These drawings appeared in *Punch* and *London Opinion* at roughly monthly intervals between July 1915 and June 1916. A thirteenth drawing, illustrating 'A Chairman Calamity' was made for use in the special Christmas Numbers of these magazines in 1915. It is interesting to note that whilst Heath Robinson had thirteen full-page cartoons published in the advertising pages of *Punch* during this one twelve-month period, the sum total of his work in the editorial sections of that magazine throughout his career amounted to only one full-page line-drawing and seven vignettes.

At about the same time that he was working on the Chairman Tobacco advertisements, in the first half of 1915, he was commissioned to make a set of six drawings showing stages in the making of Johnnie Walker whisky. The drawings illustrate testing casks, designing the label, squaring the bottles, filtering the liquor, filling bottles and testing the whisky. The approach to the drawings is similar to six cartoons that he had made for *The Sketch* some three years earlier showing the editing and production of that magazine. He had made pen-and-wash drawings of imagined manufacturing processes as early as

'Testing the Value of a Soap Advertisement', one of a series of six drawings depicting 'The Editing and Production of *The Sketch*', published in June 1912.

December 1908 when 'Kippering Herrings . . .', the first of his Great British Industries series, appeared in *The Sketch*, but this was the first time that such drawings had been commissioned for advertising. The company still owns the original drawings, but there is no record of the format in which they were first published. The fact that there are six drawings might suggest a calendar or booklet, but they might equally have appeared as a sequence of magazine advertisements, as did the 'Twelve Virtues of Chairman'.

In 1921 Heath Robinson was asked by John Mackintosh & Sons of Halifax to provide the first in a series of cartoons by famous artists showing how and where they imagine Toffee de Luxe is made. Heath Robinson called his drawing 'A half hour in Toffee Town' and with a series of six small line-drawings in a single frame showed the various stages in the toffee-making process. These included boiling, cooling, shaping, covering with chocolate, counting and testing, all conducted by solemn little men operating typical Heath Robinson machinery. Mackintosh's were delighted with the drawing. H. Mackintosh, the Managing Director, wrote to Heath Robinson: 'Since your drawing was placed before us by our Agents, Messrs T.B. Browne, Limited we have had many a good laugh over same. Knowing the real factory, we can appreciate your caricature all the more.' On Saturday 1 October 1921 the whole of the front page of the *Daily Mail* was occupied by Heath Robinson's depiction of Toffee Town, and the drawing subsequently appeared in reduced form in other periodicals. Mackintosh quickly came back for a second drawing to advertise a reduction in price of their toffee from 9d to 8d. Heath Robinson submitted a rough sketch, to which his agent reported the response as: '. . . although excellent for future use, [it is] not quite what they anticipated for "the great reduction". They expected something in your mechanical style . . .' Already he was becoming typecast, but he responded with an alternative rough sketch of a price-reduction machine complete with dials, bells and trumpets.

The 'Toffee Town' drawing was not only a success with Mackintosh, but also prompted a number of enquiries from other companies seeking similar drawings showing various stages of their manufacturing process. Discussing the price to be asked for a further drawing for Mackintosh's a year later, A.E. Johnson, Heath Robinson's agent, wrote to the artist:

We have already broached the subject of a better price, and I think possibly something may be arranged. One cannot press the point too hard, however, for it was to a great extent the first Mackintosh advertisement which brought you this later advertising business, and it's a bit hard on the firm which has the enterprise to give an artist a new opening (especially one by which the artist profits) to penalise them for the success of their own judgement.

Initially, no increase in price was negotiated, but this particular commission was the cause of some ill-feeling between artist and client. Heath Robinson was asked to make a rough sketch that the advertising agent could take to Halifax at very short notice. He met the deadline, and the drawing was passed with a

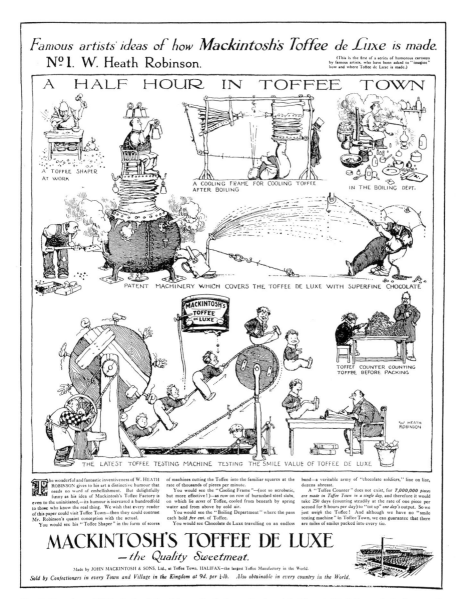

On 1 October 1921, John Mackintosh & Sons Ltd, with Heath Robinson's help, took over the front page of the *Daily Mail* to show how their Toffee de Luxe was made.

'The Latest Machine for Tipping Matches With Phosphorus', a full-page illustration from *Get on With It* (1920).

large number of amendments. The finished drawing was also required at unusually short notice and again Heath Robinson met the deadline, disrupting his programme of work in the process. He was therefore not amused when a fortnight after the 'final' deadline the drawing was returned with a request for a number of changes. Matters were made worse by the fact that he was not at all sympathetic to these changes, considering at least one of them to be 'a definite mistake'. However he effected them, and A.E. Johnson wrote a strongly worded letter to the advertising agents, informing them that an additional fee of five guineas would be charged for the alterations. He continued:

As regards the various alterations, Mr Robinson instructs me to say that the fact that he has given effect to your clients' various amendments is not to be taken as evidence that he agrees with them . . . the plausibility underlying his most extravagant inventions, which is the secret of the artist's humour, is thereby undermined. But, as Mr Heath Robinson feels it to be clear that your clients have a better notion of what a Heath Robinson drawing should look like than he has himself, he has decided to give effect to all their proposals. He does not wish them to be disappointed.

The drawing eventually appeared in the *Daily Mail* on 23 December 1922.

Amongst the requests for advertisements that followed from the 'Toffee Town' drawings were a design for Limmer & Trinidad Lake Asphalt Company, to be displayed at a trade exhibition, and a calendar design for Thomas and Green, paper makers, in a similar vein, both in full colour.

CONNOLLY LEATHER

In about 1920 Heath Robinson's younger brother George, in partnership with J. Birch, embarked on a career in publishing and advertising from offices at 17 Tooks Court, close to Chancery Lane, in London. Their first publication was *Get On With It*, a one-off magazine-style booklet designed around a series of double-page advertisements. It had a two-page introduction, sixteen full-page cartoons and 36 line-drawings by Heath Robinson in addition to one double-page and one full-page advertisement by him. A page headed 'Thoughts on Shaving Cream', with line-drawings showing what it could have done for Shylock and how it could improve Bernard Shaw, faces a drawing depicting the 'testing of shaving cream on gooseberries at one of the new Government shaving cream laboratories'. There follows a double-page coloured advertisement for McClinton's shaving soap and cream. Most of the advertisers used their standard press advertisements, but Pears and Eno commissioned drawings from Heath Robinson. Thirteen of the full-page drawings from this booklet were reissued the following year, printed in sepia and bound in a stiff card cover, under the title *Quaint and Selected Pictures*.

It was also in 1920 that Heath Robinson embarked on the second major advertising collaboration of his career, with Connolly Brothers (Curriers) Ltd, who were the largest producers of motor hides in Europe at a time when not only the seats of cars were made of leather, but also the folding hoods. They also supplied leather for furniture, bags and cases, harness and saddlery and for 'railway use'. Heath Robinson was commissioned to produce a 12-page booklet illustrating various stages in the production of Connolly motor hides for the Motor Show that year. The booklet was called *Nothing Like Leather* and contained six full pages of illustration, each with a three-quarter-page line-drawing such as 'the gent who first realised the waterproof nature of cowhide' and 'an early method of skinning a cow'. The title-page had a delightful vignette in line with the caption 'for endurance' and the cover was decorated with four silhouettes illustrating the virtues of leather. These last designs were also employed in an advertisement in an ill-fated booklet of Heath Robinson drawings called *The Home Made Car* the following year.

In 1921 Connolly's commissioned a similar booklet called *Curried Careers* from Fougasse, but this proved to be less popular. They therefore returned to Heath Robinson in 1922. The design of the second booklet was largely left to the artist, with the stipulation that it should concentrate on the motor-industry side of their trade. A.E. Johnson wrote to Heath Robinson at the end of August asking him to prepare rough sketches for a 24-page booklet, and enclosing some ideas from Denis Murphy, one of the directors, and two samples of their new 'Bedford Cord Hides' which were leather treated to look like fabric. Amongst the ideas offered were the preparation of Morocco grained hides, and the cutting of headleathers for hoods.

A dummy booklet with rough sketches was delivered to A.E. Johnson, so that he could decide with Connolly's the size and format required, and on 21 September he wrote to Heath Robinson with details. He also reluctantly advised the artist, who at the time had a very full schedule of work, that:

> . . . it will be absolutely essential for you to come up to town for half a day in order to be taken over Connolly's works again. This is most exasperating, as you are so very busy, and it seems to be totally unnecessary. But, as you know, many of these firms have an idea that nothing can be satisfactorily accomplished until you have been over the works, and the case is particularly acute with Connolly's, because the old man of the firm (a white-haired old thing whom you probably met) has got the notion *firmly* in his head, and is clinging to it with the pertinacity of the aged. I did my best to avoid the point, but I can see very clearly that if you do not pay a second visit to the works, the old man in the first place will be convinced that any and every sketch you do is not up to the standard of the first book and not nearly so good as it would have been had you again toured the works: and secondly he will develop the idea that Mr Robinson is not giving to the job as much attention as he ought to. In these circumstances there seems nothing for it but to manage another visit to the works somehow . . . Apart from its being policy to gratify the whim of old Connolly somehow, I think it will save time in the long run to fall in with his wishes. Otherwise he will be making absurd criticisms of every sketch you do, and you will lose more time over alterations, etc. than you would gain by not going.

Heath Robinson duly visited the works. On 30 September A.E. Johnson wrote to the artist with Connolly's comments on the rough sketches, most of which had been passed. The company's main concern was over the drawings at the head of the foreign-language pages at the end of the booklet, which might 'offend national susceptibilities'. They also wondered whether a more arresting picture could be produced for the front cover. Heath Robinson made the

LIGHT on LEATHER

SHED BY

W. HEATH ROBINSON

with the compliments of

CONNOLLY BROS. (CURRIERS), LTD.

Cover design for *Light on Leather*, the second booklet that Heath Robinson designed for Connolly Brothers.

25

adjustments requested and resubmitted the dummy. On Tuesday 3 October Johnson wrote to say that Connolly's were very pleased with the revised sketches, and asked for the finished drawings 'by first thing on Monday at the latest, and if by any chance you were to get them through before the end of the week, so much the better'. As usual, Heath Robinson delivered on time. Proofs of the booklet were sent on 24 October and the final product, which was called *Light on Leather* was available for distribution at the Motor Show at the beginning of November. Once again it was a success and, whilst not quite an annual institution, by 1939 the tally of Heath Robinson booklets for Connolly's was 12, including two collected editions. He also contributed to *Tough Testimonials* in 1924 which included work by ten artists.

It is difficult to select highlights from Heath Robinson's booklets for Connolly's which themselves bear witness to the sustained inventiveness and sheer brilliance of their creator. However, there are two which particularly appeal. *Nothing Takes the Place of Leather* in 1925 pictures a world without leather in which a miserable and uncomfortable populace perform various tasks with inferior substitutes. Eight years later, double in size, another classic was the *Connolly Chronicles*, in which parallels were drawn between historical events and present day uses for leather. Mr and Mrs Noah find the most comfortable seats on the Ark – on the backs of the bull and the cow – while their modern counterparts enjoy leather upholstery. Several similar parallels are illustrated in a series of finely drawn full-page and smaller pictures.

In total, Heath Robinson made over 200 drawings for Connolly Brothers, the majority of which are still in the possession of the company. For three years from 1989 they have been used to compile a series of fine calendars, each limited to 1000 copies signed by one of Heath Robinson's sons and by Tim Connolly, the present Chairman, an example of the enduring appeal of Heath Robinson's work.

ADVERTISING BOOKLETS

In 1925, Percy Bradshaw, for whom Heath Robinson had briefly worked as a tutor at his Press Art School, wrote *Art in Advertising*, a study of British and American publicity. In it he discussed the question of whether it was wise to introduce humour into advertising, especially for a company that addresses its publicity to the trade rather than to the public. However, in the example quoted any doubts were quickly set to rest. A Heath Robinson booklet, issued at a time when business was depressed and customers had forgotten how to smile, met with immediate appreciation, and further material in a similar vein not only received special mention in trade journals at home and abroad, but resulted in a great deal of business. Free editorial publicity generated by the material was in itself valuable, and the booklets even appealed to non-English-speaking customers. Before the first booklets were issued the company was faced with the obvious danger that conventional, old-fashioned traders would be offended by such frivolous advertising; but the fear was quite unfounded, as no adverse opinion or criticism of any kind was received. The company in question was Connolly Bros, but the comments could equally have applied to any of the eighty-plus companies for which Heath Robinson worked at various times.

Heath Robinson's first advertising booklet for Connolly in 1920 had been pocket-sized and contained a mere 12 pages, but the following year he was asked to illustrate a more substantial production for The Port of Manchester Warehouses. This was called *Then and Now* and was designed to promote the use of Manchester as a port by demonstrating its sophisticated modern handling and storage facilities, and to encourage companies to locate their factories on the adjacent Trafford Park Estate to take full advantage of those facilities. Heath Robinson's drawings showed his view of 'Then' whilst the 'Now' was illustrated with photographs. The first of the six full-page drawings in the book showed the 'supposed origin of the warehouse – an early effort to preserve a filbert through the winter months' and features a group of Stone Age men building the warehouse from rocks and animal skins.

The depiction of an unconventional history of the product was a frequently used approach to advertising work, being a useful alternative to the manufacturing process, or in some cases an adjunct to it. A calendar produced for Fletcher and Burrows Colliery at Atherton in Lancashire shows four stages in the mining and production of coal as it might have been in medieval times, whilst the advertisement for Sandy MacDonald Scotch Whisky published in *The Sketch* Christmas number depicts the way the whisky was distilled in the old Highland Clan days. The advertisement, in full colour, took the form of a series of small drawings like the Mackintosh's Toffee advertisement, and incorporated the authentic MacDonald tartan.

Perhaps the most complete and satisfying advertising booklet adopting a historical approach was *An Unconventional History of Hovis* published in about 1926. In its 24 pages the history of Hovis baking from the discovery of wheat in prehistoric times, through the first windmill and the first steam mill to modern methods of production and testing was recorded. The final illustration, which was also published in full colour as a magazine advertisement, contrasted the thin, sickly and fractious family that does not eat Hovis with the plump, healthy and contented inhabitants of 'The Hovis Home'. The differences extend to the cat, dog and caged bird, and even to the family's pot plants (see cover illustration).

Heath Robinson was an early broadcaster on radio, having been introduced to the medium by a competition run in April 1923 by *The Bystander*, to which he was a regular contributor. The competition was called 'Drawings by Wireless', and Heath Robinson, speaking from a studio at London's 2LO radio station, described to listeners a drawing he was making of his own radio receiver. Listeners were invited to make a similar sketch in the style of the artist and send it to *The Bystander*. A prize of 10 guineas was offered for the best entry. The following year Heath Robinson made a series of drawings for an advertising booklet published by Philips Glowlamp Works picturing *The Wireless Adventure of Mr Pimple*. The story was told in six major and six minor drawings, progressing from Mr Pimple's dream of happiness, through erection of the aerial, taking in the lead, burying the earth, finding that the completed radio yielded no sound, presentation by a friend of a Philips valve and final success. The illustrations, in the style of his children's book *Peter Quip in Search of a Friend*, are delightfully drawn, particularly the family dancing to music from the radio, making this one of the most attractive of his advertising booklets.

Perhaps the most impressive of the booklets that Heath Robinson produced are those illustrating various production processes in the construction industry. Certainly the largest is *The Wonders of Wilmington* produced for G.& T. Earle of Wilmington near Hull, manufacturers of 'Pelican' brand cement. This was hard-covered and contained five full-page illustrations finely printed on good-quality paper showing four stages in the manufacture of cement and the tests to which the finished product is subjected. The pelican which adorns the cover can also be found, looking somewhat startled, in each of the five pictures. Originally published in 1928, the same illustrations were reissued, in reduced format, as *Earle's Early Etchings* in 1949.

Only slightly less imposing in size and production quality was the booklet produced for Asbestos Cement Building Products, on *The Making of Asbestos-Cement Roofings*. This has a similar format to *The Wonders of Wilmington* with five large, well-printed illustrations showing stages in the manufacturing process, one of them spreading across two pages. Undoubtedly each of these projects required a trip to the works, and their strength lies in the closeness of the imagined processes to the real ones, notwithstanding their total absurdity, which would be recognized by knowledgable customers and add to the humour.

A more modest production relating to the construction industry is the pamphlet published by Ruston-Bucyrus of Lincoln in the late 1930s. This company manufactured mechanical excavators of various sorts, which gave full scope for Heath Robinson's more extravagant constructions. The six full-page illustrations depict two types of mechanical shovel, two varieties of dragline, a grab-crane and a skimmer. As was often the case, there is a wealth of incidental detail in the pictures. In the drawing of excavations for the foundations for a new cinema the queue for the first performance has already formed, whilst the use of a dragline to clear the upper reaches of the Thames shows an irate fishermen and fleeing bathers surprised by the operation. A variety of small line-drawings illustrate the text and show a number of new excavator designs invented by the artist.

Finally, in the field of construction, mention must be made of the booklet produced for John Booth & Sons, of Bolton, Lancs. This was called *The Problems of a Structural Engineer* and, like the one for Port of Manchester Warehouses, combined a number of drawings with photographs of recent projects undertaken by the company. Four of the full-page illustrations are divided, with the smaller top portion showing a problem, and the lower portion its solution using Booth's structural steel. The re-roofing of a weaving-shed to eliminate a forest of columns is particularly interesting, since it offers no scope for mechanical extravagance, and has been treated in the manner of the Hovis advertisement. The scene before shows harassed and unfashionably dressed employees operating antiquated machinery amid a confusion of columns in an untidy and uncomfortable old weaving-shed. Below is a picture of the new weaving-shed with a Booth's 'warren-girder' roof eliminating the need for supporting columns. Fashionably dressed, smiling young ladies operate the latest machinery in their spacious and orderly work area. Baskets of flowers hang from the roof, a carpeted aisle terminates at a plinth surmounted by an aspidistra, and work is directed by frock-coated managers. An open box of chocolates is placed on an occasional table and a weary employee rests on a comfortable Chesterfield.

LATER WORK

In 1930 Heath Robinson was one of the artists invited to contribute to the decoration of *The Empress of Britain*, a new luxury liner being built on the Clyde for the Canadian Pacific Railway Company (CPR). Writing about this project, the editor of *The Studio* said in 1931:

In constructing the latest and biggest addition to their fleet the CPR have succeeded in presenting to the world an exhibition of the concerted efforts of British talent and

The Knickerbocker Bar on the transatlantic liner *Empress of Britain*.

In 1935 the Great Western Railway celebrated its centenary with the publication of *Railway Ribaldry* – 96 pages of railway humour by W. Heath Robinson.

British manufacture. Seldom, in recent times, can one point to a more successful example of what Britain stands for in fine quality of material linked with superb craftsmanship and engineering.

Heath Robinson was responsible for the decoration of the children's room and the cocktail bar, and his drawings were painted on large wooden panels in his studio. The main designs for the cocktail bar showed the story of cocktails, and these were supplemented by a number of circular *trompe l'oeil* panels in the ceiling showing faces looking down, a parachutist dropping in, or a ramshackle aeroplane passing overhead. The decorations formed the basis of an article by Anthony Armstrong called 'The Story of Cocktails' which was published in *The Strand Magazine* in December 1931 and was reprinted by CPR as an advertising brochure. In 1938 the same set of illustrations was used in *Cocktail Mixing*, a small, 12-page booklet containing a number of cocktail recipes.

Heath Robinson's largest single promotional commission came from the Great Western Railway in 1935, when it published *Railway Ribaldry*, a book of 45 full-page and 52 smaller line-drawings, to celebrate its centenary. This book, unlike the majority of Heath Robinson's publicity material, was put on general sale at a shilling, and so very large numbers of copies were distributed. The book displays the full range of the artist's invention, from the history of railways, through eccentric manufacturing processes, novel ways of operating a railway and new methods of training the staff, to the peculiarities of its customers. The book was produced in card covers, but a small number of copies were bound in paper-covered boards for presentation to customers and associates of the company.

Towards the end of 1935, Heath Robinson was asked to make some drawings to be used in advertisements for Douglas Stuart, a leading London bookmaker. His approach to this commission is of particular interest, since his mechanical inventions were inappropriate to the subject, as was a historical treatment. He chose instead to revive the method of working that he had used in his earliest advertising commissions with Potter and Evans. This was to take a catchphrase and to illustrate it in a humorous way, often by taking an over-literal interpretation of the words used. Each of the drawings that he made had one or more horses in it, and references to putting 'your shirt' or 'a monkey' on a horse inspired some of the artist's most inventive and witty drawings of his later years. A total of eight drawings were published between January 1936 and April 1937, appearing on the back covers of the *Illustrated Sporting and Dramatic News* and the *Illustrated London News*, and most were used two or three times.

Heath Robinson always paid great attention to the details of clothing in his drawings, to the extent that it is possible to date some of them by the ladies fashions, particularly in hats. It was therefore appropriate that he should be called on to provide publicity material for leading gentlemen's outfitters. The first such commission seems to have been a drawing made for the tailors Hector Powe sometime before 1925 called 'The History of a Pair of Trousers'. This is

'All the Best for 1940', Heath Robinson's advertising supplement in the 1940 New Year issue of the *Evening Standard*, included his distinctive view of Burberrys' tailoring.

described by Percy Bradshaw in *Art in Advertising* as having been published in *Pow Wow*, the company's house magazine, but no copy of this has yet been traced. More accessible are the set of drawings made for a New York outfitters, the Rogers Peet Company, for a booklet entitled *Some Trade Secrets Revealed*. Two of these drawings were reproduced in the US magazine *Printed Salesmanship* in June 1927, and the full set of six in *The Gentle Art of Advertising*, the collection compiled by Quentin Robinson for Duckworth in 1979. (This collection also included all but one of the drawings prepared for the booklet *Behind the Scenes at Moss Bros.* in 1936.) Finally, in 1940, an advertisement in the *Evening Standard* for Burberrys stressed the individual and personal attention accorded to their clients by showing fifteen or more staff engaged in measuring a single customer. It was a sign of the times that in the background a number of men were shown trying on new military uniforms.

The Burberrys advertisement appeared in one of a series of New Year advertising supplements that featured in the first issue of the *Evening Standard* published in most years between 1932 and 1940. In total there were seven such supplements, of which Heath Robinson supplied the drawings for four (Bert Thomas, Gilbert Wilkinson and Ridgewell undertaking one each). The supplements occupied between one and two pages of the paper, and consisted of a pictorial title-piece over quarter-page line-drawings advertising various products. The same products often appeared from year to year, the most regular being Nugget boot polish, Smith's Sectric clocks and Wright's coal-tar soap.

Heath Robinson's last advertising commission came in 1941 when he was invited to make a series of pen-and-wash illustrations of flying terms under the general heading 'The War In the Air' for High Duty Alloys of Slough. At the time he was making a weekly drawing for *The Sketch* and these drawings, which were published in *Flight* and *The Aeroplane*, are in a similar vein. Copies of the earlier drawings could be obtained by writing to the company, but this offer was discontinued later in the series, presumably because of the paper shortage.

At the time of his death in 1944 only a minority of Heath Robinson's public remembered his work as a serious illustrator, but like Hogarth and Rowlandson before him the appeal of his humorous art was largely the result of his considerable talents as a serious artist. He was unusually prolific, with a seemingly inexhaustible stock of good ideas. The basis of his humour was human nature, and so the majority of his work seems as fresh and relevant today as when it was first published. The artist is no longer with us, but his spirit lives on in his gentle and perceptive humour.

That Heath Robinson's drawings are still being used in advertising, either to promote the products for which they were originally intended, or in new and original ways, supports the statement by Christopher Mann in *Commercial Art* in 1927 that:

. . . the gigantic absurdity of Robinson has as much to do with business as that other seeming irrelevance of a good lunch. It induces a favourable disposition of mind, a

Four good resolutions that were suggested to readers of the New Year issue of the *Evening Standard* in 1939.

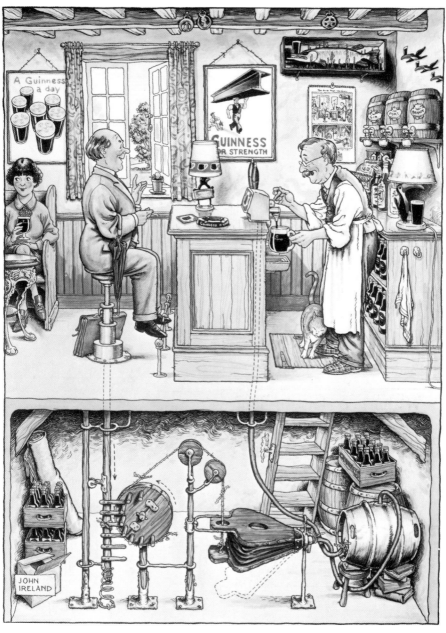

John Ireland's idea of how Heath Robinson, assisted by his cat, Saturday Morning, might have served a pint of draught Guinness.

mellowing of the temper, an inclination to listen and agree. His drawings prove that the world will not only laugh with you if you are really amusing but also put its hand in its pocket and buy what you have to sell.

The greatest compliment of all was paid to his enduring worth in advertising by Guinness in 1981. Having omitted to secure Heath Robinson's services during his lifetime, they employed the distinguished artist John Ireland to make a set of 12 full-colour drawings for a calendar in his style. These clever drawings capture the spirit of Heath Robinson's work, the last of them showing the great man himself, complete with carpet slippers and cat, drawing a pint of Guinness for a customer, in a bar decorated with a range of earlier Guinness advertising ephemera. The front cover of this calendar bears the legend 'An affectionate evocation of the work of W. Heath Robinson.'

Geoffrey Beare is a well-known authority on the works of W. Heath Robinson, of which he has been a collector since 1971. He is the author of *The Illustrations of W. Heath Robinson*, which is the definitive guide to the artist's more serious output. His most recent publication was the catalogue for a major exhibition of pictures by all three Robinson brothers at Chris Beetles Ltd in London.

THE TWELVE VIRTUES OF CHAIRMAN

THE TWELVE VIRTUES OF CHAIRMAN.
No. 1.—Attractive Aroma.

DARING AIR RAID IN THE SUBURBS.

St. John's Wood telegram, 7 p.m., reports well-known resident enjoying evening pipe at upper window suddenly surprised by airman who took pipe and vanished.

8 p.m. Assumed that airman was attracted by aroma of the tobacco.

Later. Tobacco ascertained to be Chairman.

Chairman is a fine tobacco, cool, pleasing and fragrant. It is made in different strengths to meet the tastes of most men—" Chairman," medium; " Boardman's," mild; and " Recorder," full—and is packed in 1 and 2 oz. lead packets and $\frac{1}{4}$, $\frac{1}{2}$ and 1 lb. tins, and sold at 6d. per oz. by all tobacconists and stores in the British Isles.

Also sold by principal dealers in Canada, Australia, New Zealand, India, Egypt, S. Africa, France, Norway & Sweden.

R. J. LEA, LIMITED, MANCHESTER.

THE TWELVE VIRTUES OF CHAIRMAN.

No. 2.—A solace to the very end.

A pipe of Chairman is a solace to the very end. It smokes cool and sweet and with a pleasing fragrance to the last shre !—the last whiff.

It is a comfort in times of stress; a help in times of trouble and a cheery friend on all occasions. Whether smoked much or little it is always the same—always pleasing, always satisfactory.

The wise man who smokes it has in it the best that tobacco can give—a higher price could not improve it or a lower one provide it.

It is Chairman—a fine tobacco.

It is made in different strengths to meet the tastes of most men—"Chairman," medium; "Boardman's," mild; and "Recorder," full — and is packed in 1 and 2 oz. lead packets and ¼, ½ and 1 lb. tins, and sold at 6d. per oz. by all tobacconists and stores in the British Isles.

Also sold by principal dealers in Canada, Australia, New Zealand, India, Egypt, S. Africa, France, Norway and Sweden.

R. J. LEA, LIMITED, MANCHESTER.

THE TWELVE VIRTUES OF CHAIRMAN.
No. 3.—Entire absence of burning sensation.

When preparing for a dinner you have no wish to attend the wonderful coolness of Chairman is most comforting—as welcome to the smoker as it is unexpected by those who do not know it.

Those who smoke Chairman have the best that tobacco can give, and to those who newly try it it brings an unlooked for pleasure, as its continued enjoyment is not gained at the cost of a burned tongue.

In all ways it is a fine tobacco, with a pleasing aroma, an attractive flavour, and a peculiar coolness that is as un-usual as it is essential to the complete enjoyment of the pipe.

It is made in different strengths to meet the tastes of most men—"Chairman," medium; "Boardman's," mild; and "Recorder," full—and is packed in one and 2 oz. lead packets and ¼, ½, and 1-lb. tins, and sold at 6d. per oz. by all tobacconists and stores in the British Isles.

Also sold by principal dealers in Canada, Australia, New Zealand, India, Egypt, S. Africa, France, Norway and Sweden.

R. J. LEA, LIMITED, MANCHESTER.

THE TWELVE VIRTUES OF CHAIRMAN.
No. 4.—Fragrance which all enjoy.

The smoking of Chairman is a kindly and pleasing habit, gratifying to others as well as to the smoker himself. Those who are barred from its direct enjoyment can share its pleasures when opportunity permits.

With it the pipe is no longer banned from sitting-room and lounge nor consigned to the outer darkness of the garden or the solitude of the study.

Its pleasing flavour and fine fragrance may be enjoyed on all occasions when the pipe is permissible and always with satisfaction, for it does not burn the tongue.

It is made in different strengths to meet the tastes of most men—"Chairman," medium; "Boardman's," mild; and "Recorder," full — and is sold at 8d. per oz. in 1 and 2 oz. lead packets, and at 2/7 per ½-lb. in ¼, ½ and 1 lb. tins, by all leading tobacconists and stores.

Also sold by principal dealers in Canada, Australia, New Zealand, India, Egypt, S. Africa, France, Norway and Sweden.

R. J. LEA, LIMITED, MANCHESTER.

THE TWELVE VIRTUES OF CHAIRMAN.
No. 5.—Its soothing properties.

It is an open question what the opinion of the guardian of the law may be, but there is no room for doubt that the substantial special and the distracted parent well know the soothing properties of Chairman.

At anxious and worrying times a pipe of this fine tobacco has a most calming effect on all who come within the influence of its gracious aroma.

The man who smokes it enjoys the best that tobacco has to give. Its pleasing flavour appeals to the palate with every pipe, for it smokes sweet and cool to the last shred. It does not burn the tongue or worry the throat however much it may be smoked.

A delightful aroma—a pleasing flavour—an intense and unusual coolness—a pleasure with every pipe—that is Chairman.

It is made in different strengths to meet the tastes of most men—"Chairman," medium; "Boardman's," mild; and "Recorder," full—and is sold at 8d. per oz. in 1 and 2 oz. lead packets, and at 2/7 per ¼-lb. in ¼, ½ and 1-lb. tins by all principal tobacconists and stores.

Also sold by principal dealers in Canada, Australia, New Zealand, India, Egypt, S. Africa, France. Norway, Sweden, and the Far East.

R. J. LEA, LIMITED, MANCHESTER.

THE TWELVE VIRTUES OF CHAIRMAN.
No. 6.—Promotes geniality.

The virtues of Chairman are very real. It is most improbable that the genial and friendly feeling depicted above, or even the good fellowship of less unusual occasions, would be born of a poor or ordinary tobacco. The right atmosphere is created only by the best that tobacco has to give. That is Chairman.

And there is economy in it also. The difference in cost between Chairman and an ordinary tobacco—even a low-priced tobacco—is a few pence a week at the most. But the difference in satisfaction is so much greater that it far outweighs this small extra cost. It means an added pleasure with every pipe. Hours of it. Actually about six hours to the ounce, which makes Chairman one of the least costly but most real and satisfying of the little pleasures of life.

Chairman is medium in strength, with a pleasing flavour and aroma and always cool to the tongue. Boardman's is the same tobacco milder, and Recorder the same but fuller flavoured.

These three brands are sold by all leading tobacconists and stores at 8d. per oz. in 1 and 2 oz. lead packets, and at 2/7 per ¼-lb. in ¼, ½ and 1-lb. tins.

Also sold by principal dealers in France, Norway, Sweden, India, Canada, Egypt, S. Africa New Zealand, and the Far East.

R. J. LEA LIMITED, MANCHESTER.

43

THE TWELVE VIRTUES OF CHAIRMAN.

No. 7.—It steadies the nerves.

A golfing lie at times calls for a heavy mashie, whilst at others it needs much swallowing. The artist has depicted a third kind that includes these two and also emphasises the need of that most desirable quality—steadiness of the nerves.

Golfers generally are smokers. The golfing temperament is fostered by the soothing and calming properties of such a fine tobacco as Chairman, as it is an intensely cool mixture, which smokes evenly and sweetly to the last shred, giving a delightful aroma and most pleasing flavour all the while.

It is finely blended, giving to the smoker with every pipe the best that tobacco has to give. It does not either burn or bite the tongue, nor does its constant use diminish the enjoyment in it.

And its use is a most inexpensive luxury. Each ounce gives a full six hours' enjoyment.

It is made in different strengths to meet the tastes of most men—"Chairman," medium; "Boardman's," mild; and "Recorder," full—and is sold at 8d. per oz. in 1 and 2 oz. lead packets, and at 2/7 per ¼-lb. in ¼, ½ and 1-lb. tins by all principal tobacconists and stores.

Also sold by principal dealers in Canada, Australia, New Zealand, India, Egypt, S. Africa France, Norway, Sweden, and the Far East.

R. J. LEA, LIMITED, MANCHESTER.

THE TWELVE VIRTUES OF CHAIRMAN.

No. 8.—Its Taking Qualities.

The taking qualities of Chairman are unusual in their excellence. When smoked it burns with an aroma as pleasing to others as to the smoker himself, and it yields a flavour that appeals with every pipe. But its most unusual feature is its coolness, which makes the enjoyment of it constant; it does not burn or bite the tongue however much it may be smoked.

Its charming aroma makes it a tobacco particularly suitable for indoors smoking and, at the present time its price makes it one of the most inexpensive of pleasures, as an ounce packet yields a full six hours of enjoyable smoking.

It is made in different strengths to meet the tastes of most men—" Chairman," medium ; " Boardman's," mild ; and " Recorder," full—and is sold at 8d. per oz. in 1 and 2 oz. lead packets, and at 2/7 per ¼-lb. in ¼, ½ and 1-lb. tins by all principal tobacconists and stores.

Also sold by principal dealers in Canada, Australia, New Zealand, India, Egypt, S. Africa, France, Norway, Sweden and the Far East.

R. J. LEA, LIMITED, MANCHESTER.

45

THE TWELVE VIRTUES OF CHAIRMAN.

No. 9.—Banishes Discomfort and brings Content.

A pipe of Chairman is most excellent smoking at all times, but never are its virtues more potent than when discomfort reigns—its soothing influence brings a cheerful content in its train. It pleases the palate with its flavour and its clean and fragrant aroma is a delight which others than the smoker may enjoy.

The pleasures it gives are constant with every pipe no matter how much it may be smoked, as it is always cool to the tongue and burns sweetly to the last shred.

In these days of higher taxation it is an economy, as it costs less than either cigars or cigarettes of satisfying quality.

Each ounce yields a full six hours of enjoyment and costs but eightpence.

It is made in different strengths to meet the tastes of most men—" Chairman," medium; " Boardman's," mild; and " Recorder," full—and is sold at 8d. per oz. in 1 and 2 oz. lead packets, and at 2/7 per ¼-lb. in ¼, ½ and 1-lb. tins by all principal tobacconists and stores.

Also sold by principal dealers in Canada, Australia, New Zealand, India, Egypt, S. Africa, France, Norway, Sweden and the Far East.

R. J. LEA, LIMITED, MANCHESTER.

W
HEATH
ROBINSON

THE TWELVE VIRTUES OF CHAIRMAN.

No. 10.—It suits most palates.

There is a very unusual attractiveness about Chairman. It pleases the palate with its coolness and flavour, and it has an aroma which appeals to most people whether they are smokers or not. As a pipe tobacco it has no superior.

Also at the present time, especially, it is an economy, being cheaper than either cigarettes or cigars of a quality which can possibly satisfy, as it provides six hours of the best smoking to the ounce.

It is made in different strengths to meet the tastes of most men—" Chairman," medium ; " Boardman's," mild ; and " Recorder," full—and is sold at 8d. per oz. in 1 and 2 oz. lead packets, and at 2/7 per ¼-lb. in ¼, ½ and 1-lb. tins by all principal tobacconists and stores.

Also sold by principal dealers in Canada, Australia, New Zealand, India, Egypt, S. Africa, France, Norway, Sweden and the Far East.

R. J. LEA, LIMITED, MANCHESTER.

47

THE TWELVE VIRTUES OF CHAIRMAN.

No. 11.—It promotes Mark Tapleyism.

When through unkind circumstances one is plunged into the midst of troubles, a pipe of Chairman is very comforting. It buoys up the feelings, and helps one to take a more cheerful view of things. For it is a fine tobacco that yields the greatest pleasure that the votary of the pipe may experience. It is cool to the tongue, fragrant in its burning, and with a flavour that pleases with every pipe. It neither palls on the palate nor loses its charm, but is a sure source of pleasure month in and month out.

At the present time it is especially an economy, yielding six hours of the best smoking to the ounce.

It is made in different strengths to meet the tastes of most men—" Chairman," medium ; " Boardman's," mild ; and " Recorder," full—and is sold at 8d. per oz. in 1 and 2 oz. lead packets, and at 2/7 per ¼-lb. in ¼, ½ and 1-lb. canisters by all principal tobacconists and stores.

Also sold by principal dealers in Canada, Australia, New Zealand, India, Egypt, S. Africa, France, Norway, Sweden and the Far East.

R. J. LEA, LIMITED, MANCHESTER.

THE TWELVE VIRTUES OF CHAIRMAN.
No. 12.—It is an economy.

Chairman goes twice as far as an ordinary tobacco. This is due to its perfect combustion. It burns slowly and evenly to the last shred. The pipe is the most economical form of smoking—Chairman is the most economical of pipe tobaccos. Each ounce yields a full six hours of enjoyment and costs but eightpence.

And it has other fine qualities—it pleases the palate with its flavour and its clean and fragrant aroma is a delight which others than the smoker may enjoy.

The pleasures it gives are constant with every pipe, no matter how much it may be smoked, as it is always cool to the tongue.

It is made in different strengths to meet the tastes of most men—" Chairman," medium ; " Boardman's," mild ; and " Recorder," full—and is sold at 8d. per oz. in 1 and 2 oz. lead packets, and at 2/7 per ¼-lb. in ¼, ½ and 1-lb. canisters by all principal tobacconists and stores.

Also sold by principal dealers in Canada, Australia, New Zealand, India, Egypt, S. Africa, France, Norway, Sweden and the Far East.

R. J. LEA, LIMITED, MANCHESTER.

Chairman Calamity.

This is the wholly misleading drawing that the artist supplied. His collaborator, the man of words and phrases, would have nothing to do with it. It worried him. He could not find a useful argument for his purpose in the tubby turbot, the confiding crab or the savoury sardine. Nor did the submersible smoker, the curious chicken—or should it be the searching seagull?—inspire him with words to convey the fact that the illustration is intended to emphasise the perfect combustion of Chairman.

So it is left for the commercial man to say that this quality is responsible for the intense and delightful coolness of his tobacco, and ensures its delicate flavour and pleasing aroma being enjoyed with every pipe, however much it may be smoked.

Chairman Tobacco is made in three strengths— "Chairman," medium; "Boardman's," mild; "Recorder," full—and is sold by all leading tobacconists and stores at 8d. per ounce in 1 and 2 oz. lead packets, and 2s. 7d. per ¼-lb., in ¼, ½, and 1 lb. tins.

Also sold by principal dealers in France, Norway, Sweden, India, Canada, Egypt, South Africa, Australia, New Zealand, and the East.

R. J. LEA LIMITED, MANCHESTER.

JOHNNIE WALKER

The Johnnie Walker Experts Testing Whisky Samples With the Patent Testing Dial in the Sample Room

In the Johnnie Walker Filling Cellars

In the Filtering Vaults at Kilmarnock

54

Squareing the Johnnie Walker Bottles

Designing the Well-known Get-up of Johnnie Walker in the Johnnie Walker Studios

The Johnnie Walker Cask Expert Testing the Soundness of a Cask

It's Thirsty Work!

(Advertisement for Barclay's Lager)

NOTHING LIKE LEATHER

For Endurance

LEATHER CATCHERS ON
THE BANKS OF THE
WANDLE

W. HEATH ROBINSON

KIDNAPPING LEATHER

60

SHAVING
LEATHER

W. HEATH
ROBINSON

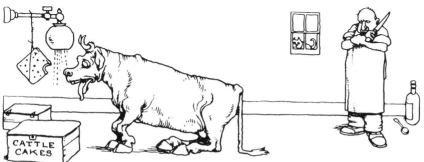

CATTLE
CAKES

GASSING A COW BEFORE
REMOVING THE HIDE

ENCOURAGING
FLEXIBILITY IN LEATHER

BOILING OIL, AND
SOAKING AND
DRYING LEATHER

W. HEATH ROBINSON.

FILLING UP WARBLE
HOLES

STOVING

ENAMEL

THE LATEST PROCESS FOR
EMBOSSING & ENAMELLING LEATHER

W. HEATH ROBINSON

SPLITTING HIDES

*An early method of
skinning a cow*

THEN AND NOW

How the Inventor of the Refrigerating Process First Discovered the Preservative
Properties of Ice

Supposed Origin of the Warehouse
An early effort to preserve a filbert through the winter months.

Congestion Arising from Manhandling

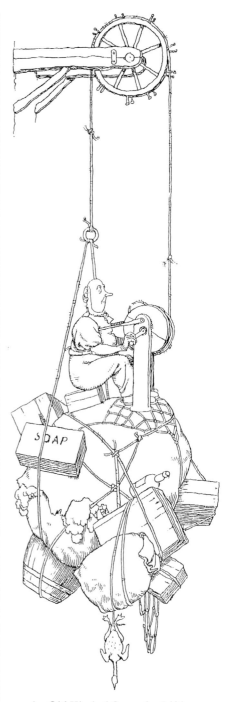

An Early Crane
*A cave man's method of bringing up
his wife's breakfast.*

An Old Kind of Crane for Lifting
General Stores into the Warehouse

70

Sectional View of Old-Fashioned Manhandled Warehouse With Storeys

One of the Evil Effects of
Manhandling Starch in Rainy
Weather

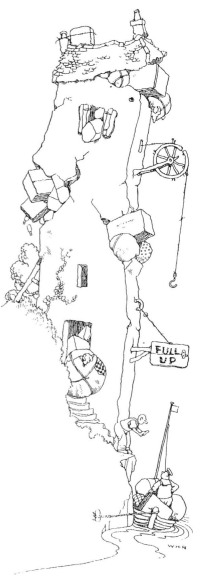

Lack of Accommodation in an
Old-fashioned Warehouse

One of the Old Machines for Counting and Checking Peas After Haulage

An Old and Somewhat Laborious Method of Refrigerating a Fresh Herring

A Dream of the Future

Some Difficulties Noah Had to Contend With in Storing for the Rainy Season

THE LIGHT SIDE OF PHOTOGRAPHY

Wedding Group Photography

Some simple and original suggestions for photographing the party without unduly embarrassing the bride and bridegroom

Hints to Golfers

How to get a natural and unaffected snap of yourself at the crucial moment.

Photography on the Cricket Field

How instructive snaps may be taken of the actual play on the cricket field.

Seaside Photography

A simple method of securing pleasing snapshots of Channel swimmers and others.

Animal Photography

Some simple devices for securing interesting snaps of animal life with rustic backgrounds.

On the River

The simplest and surest methods of securing snapshots of river scenes.

Big Game Photography

How to snap big game in its native haunts.

Child Photography

How to snap baby with a really pleased expression.

At Home Photography

A simple device for taking a snap of Grandpa with a genial and kindly expression and suitable background. (NB This method is not guaranteed to produce results in the USA, but the effect of lime juice might be tried.)

Hints for Christmas

How to take a flashlight of the Xmas Dinner Party.

11.55 pm on 31 December

How to take the very first snap of the New Year.

HOW IT IS DONE!

The manufacture of cotton fabrics according to Heath Robinson—the famous humorist

"A little nonsense now and then is relished by the wisest men."

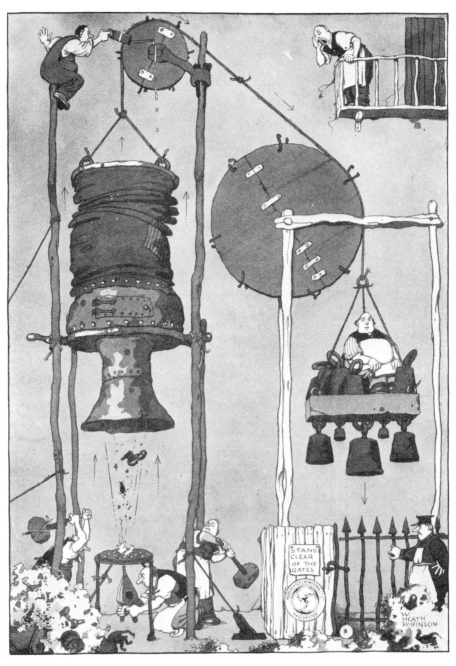

Beating Out and Drawing Out Impurities from Raw Cotton

Cotton Spinning as Performed by Spinsters

A Delightfully Ingenious Method of Weaving with Patent Scooter Shuttle

THE FIRST COLLIERY

Just Up

An old-fashioned miner leaving work.

The Pit Head

The Pit (sectional view)

Screening and Picking Coal

A Busy Day in the Washery

Old Method of Totalling Cash Sales

(Advertisement for Burroughs Adding Machines Ltd)

IZAL KILLS GERMS

The Afterglow of an Izal Bath

In the Tax Collector's Office

In School

In Court

In the Office

101

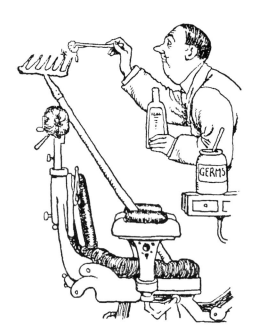

In the Dental Surgery

ENTICING A
DELICATE BEE
TO AN IZAL
DISINFECTING
FOUNTAIN

On the Bee Farm

AN INGENIOUS APPARATUS FOR DISINFECTING A BROODY HEN

On the Poultry Farm

In Church

On the Stock Farm

In the Surgery

Latest equipment for the treatment of wounds.

THE WIRELESS ADVENTURES OF MR PIMPLE

Mr. Pimple's dream of happiness.

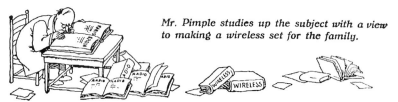

Mr. Pimple studies up the subject with a view
to making a wireless set for the family.

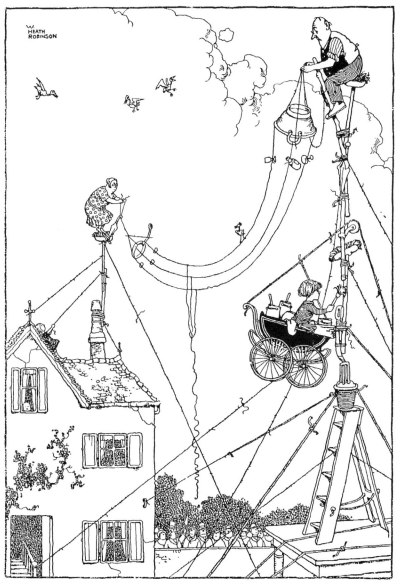

Mr. Pimple begins with the aerial — not forgetting a coat of paint.

Mr. Pimple is ingenious and finds a use for everything.

Taking the lead in (magnetic method).

Nothing comes amiss.

Even making a hole in the wall for the earth wire presents no difficulty to Mr. Pimple.

Mr. Pimple now carefully earths the earth wire.

At last everything is ready, but alas, no result is obtained.

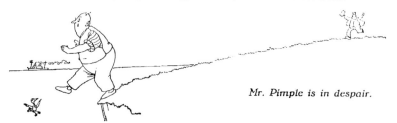

Mr. Pimple is in despair.

– until a true friend in need arrives and presents him with a real remedy for his troubles.

W·HEATH ROBINSON

Mr. Pimple now buys Philips' Receiving Valves every time and discovers that they give the very best results.

Osram Valves – A Tonic to Any Set!

(Advertisement for Osram Valves, General Electric Co. Ltd)

NOTHING TAKES THE PLACE OF LEATHER

A Sad Accident Through Using a
Cheap Substitute for Leather

If There Were No Leather Motor Hoods

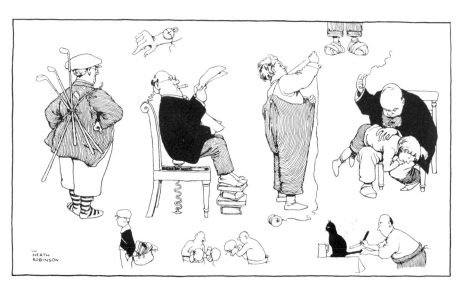

Doing Without Leather in the Home

114

If There Were No Leather Bags

A Bootless Game

The Leather-less Hunting Field

AN UNCONVENTIONAL HISTORY OF HOVIS

W HEATH ROBINSON

The Discovery of Wheat

Primitive Methods of Cutting and Threshing the Wild Corn

The First Millstones

Some prehistoric methods of grinding and pounding the hard corn for convenience in making dough for cakes etc etc.

The Landing of the Romans in Ancient Britain

The Ancient Britons Having Received Some Useful Tips from the Romans, Soon Got into the Way of Baking their Own Cakes

The First Windmill

The First Steam Mill

Busy Times in the Hovis Testing Laboratories

Interior of Modern Bakery

126

SOME TRADE SECRETS REVEALED

Clans of MacRogers and MacPeet Rounding up Mist for Rogers Peet's Scotch Mist
Cloth

Subjecting Cloth to Rogers Peet's Ingenious Sheep Dog Test for All Wool

A Busy Afternoon in the Weighing Yards of Rogers Peet's Solight Hat Department

Obtaining Style Reactions at the Monthly Meeting of the Rogers Peet Company's
Board of Directors

Research work by Rogers Peet's Expert Detectives to Obtain Data on Which to Base
their Famous 85 Percenter Last for Shoes

Up-to-date Tie Tests Employed by Messrs Rogers Peet Company

Heath Robinson's Idea of Comfort
(Advertisement for Comfort Soap, Lever Bros Ltd)

THE MAKING OF ASBESTOS CEMENT ROOFING

A Patent Double-Action Grinder for Mashing the Asbestos Fibre

The Mining and Transport of Raw Asbestos

Efficient Plant for the Successful Mixing of Treated Asbestos Fibre with Cement

Powerful Machinery for Conducting the Mixture to the Cylindrical Sieves for Draining off the Water . . .

. . . Whence a Thin Film is Conveyed to the Cylinder Upon Which the Sheet is Built, and this Finally to the Cutting Machine

An Interesting Afternoon in the Finishing Departments of an Asbestos Cement Factory

CONNOLLY CHRONICLES

1066   1933

LEATHER'S ALWAYS LEATHER

History Repeats Itself

History Repeats Itself

History Repeats Itself

WILLIAM THE CONQUEROR
APPRECIATES THE COMFORTS OF
LEATHER WHEN CROSSING THE CHANNEL

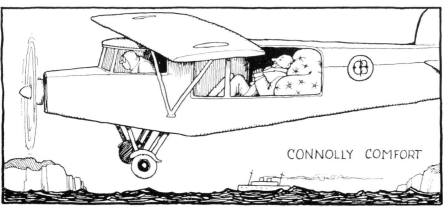

CONNOLLY COMFORT

History Repeats Itself

History Repeats Itself

146

DRAKE IS IN HIS HAMMOCK
—A THOUSAND MILE AWAY

W HEATH ROBINSON

CONNOLLY AND CLIMATE.

History Repeats Itself

WHEN JULIUS CAESAR FIRST
STEPPED ASHORE ON THE
BANKS OF THE WANDLE

COCKTAIL MIXING

Naming New Cocktails

Grading and Picking Cherries

Stoning Cherries

150

A Pleasant Surprise

The Cocktail in the Far East

Polishing Cherries

Putting the Sticks Into Cherries

Testing a New Brew

In the Clouds

Sky High

Cocktail Kindness

Saved From Suicide

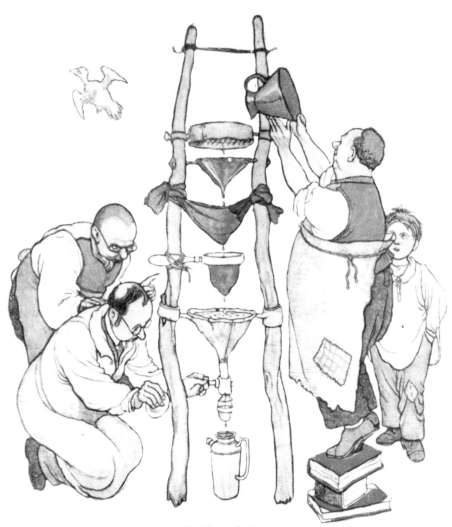

Clarifying Cocktails

Cocktail Courage

156

TELL 'DUGGIE'
ALL ABOUT IT

There's Absolutely No Limit to What You Can Put On a Horse

If You Want to Be In On a Good Double Event

When You're Putting Your Shirt on a Horse

When Backing a Horse in Your Own Home

When Getting a Tip Straight from the Horse's Mouth

If You Are About to Put a 'Monkey' On a Horse

If You Must Have Something On

THE GENTLE ART OF EXCAVATING

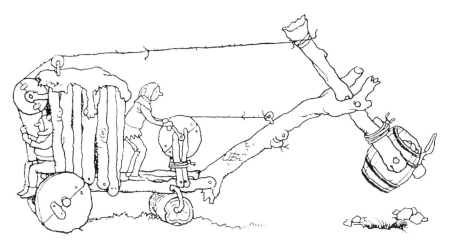

The Inventor of the Mechanical Shovel Trying Out an Early Type

AN IMPROVED
DRAGLINE
CLEARING OUT THE
BOTTOM OF THE
UPPER REACHES OF
THE RIVER THAMES

166

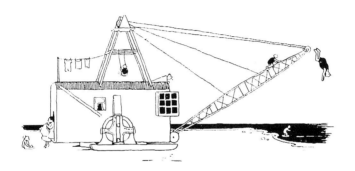

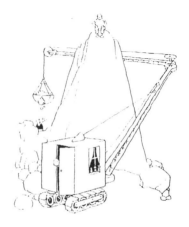

AN EARLY FORM OF THE **WALKING DRAGLINE** STRIPPING ROCKY OVERBURDEN PREPARATORY TO ERECTING A NEW TEA SHOP IN THE ALLEGHANY MOUNTAINS

A Lincolnshire Handicap
An annual sporting event on the Ruston-Bucyrus test ground.

POT POURRI

(Advertisement for Youngman ladders)

Two advertisements for Continental Ballon Tyres, Continental Tyre Co., Germany

(Advertisement for High Duty Alloys, Ltd)

THE ROAD TO COLCHIS

How I think Jason must have won the Golden Fleece

(*Advertisement from* The Silver Fox Argosy, *The Nithsdale Silver Fox Ranch*)

(Advertisement for Bryant & May Ltd)

(From The Art of Papermaking *calendar, Thomas & Green Ltd)*

(From Zerkall Bütten Auf Der Maschine Geschopft, *Zerkall Bütten, Germany)*

BIBLIOGRAPHY

This bibliography sets out to list all of W. Heath Robinson's drawings and watercolours that were commissioned and published for advertising and publicity purposes. By its nature such material is ephemeral, and much of it was only circulated within narrow trade circles. There is no national archive for such material, as there is for books and periodicals, and many of the companies that originally commissioned the work have ceased trading or been absorbed into larger conglomerates. It is therefore inevitable that the listing is incomplete, and the author would welcome any additional information that readers can supply.

The present listing would be less complete than it is were it not for the earlier efforts of others on which it has been possible to build, and access to private archives and collections. In particular I must express gratitude to the late Quentin Robinson, who compiled *The Gentle Art of Advertising* published by Duckworth in 1979; to Mr J.-P. Marix Evans, formerly chairman of Lamson Industries (UK) Ltd, for giving up a great deal of time to explain the early history of the Lamson Paragon companies and for granting access to material relating to those companies and to Chas Ed Potter; to Anthony Hussey for giving unlimited access to the Connolly Bros archives; to Simon Heneage for suggesting additional items for this listing; and to Mr Austin Reeve for making available the results of his earlier researches into Heath Robinson's advertising work.

The items in the bibliography are listed in alphabetical order of the company commissioning the work. The sizes given are page sizes with the page height given first.

179

Asbestos Cement Building Products

1. *The Making of Asbestos Cement Roofing* as seen by W. Heath Robinson, Asbestos Cement Building Products, Trafford Park, Manchester, nd.
356 × 254 mm, 16 pp.
Grey boards printed in black and blue, tied with a grey ribbon.
Six full-page half-tone illustrations.
Illustrated: *My Line of Life*, facing p. 178.
The Gentle Art of Advertising, Duckworth, 1979 pp. 79–82.

Barclay's Lager

2. 'Its Thirsty Work.'
Full-page press advertisement in line.
Published: *Punch*, 7 Apr. 1926, p. xxi.

Barford & Perkins Ltd

3. 'The New Model Type WHY4 Roller.'
Press advertisement in line, nd.
Illustrated: *The Gentle Art of Advertising*, p. 86.

Bassetts Birmingham Asphalt Ltd

4. *Greetings From Macadam*, Christmas card, 1921.
Four pages with two full-page drawings in two colours on the outside and a double-page line-drawing inside.

Bayliss, Jones & Bayliss Ltd

5. *Nibal Fencing And Wrought Iron Gates*.
Three rough sketches, possibly for a booklet, for Bayliss, Jones & Bayliss Ltd, Wolverhampton, entitled:
a. Notes on Nibal Fencing
b. Testing the unclimbability of 'Nibal' fencing.
c. How wrought iron gates are wrought.
It is not known whether this project proceeded to completion.
Illustrated: *A History of G.K.N.* by Dr Edgar Jones, vol. II, pp. 223–5.

John Booth & Sons

6. *Problems of a Structural Engineer* by W. Heath Robinson, with a foreword by Ashley Sterne. John Booth & Sons, Bolton, Lancashire, nd (*c.* 1930).
290 × 201 mm, 24 pp.

Pictorial wrappers.
Seven full-page half-tone illustrations and eight smaller drawings in line.

Bryant & May Ltd

7. 'Testing Safety Matches.'
Full-page press advertisement in line.
Published: *The Humorist*, 29 Jan. 1927, p. 697.
Illustrated: *The Gentle Art of Advertising*, p. 83.

Burberrys Ltd

8. 'Burberrys New Year's Slogan: Quality – Individual and Personal Attention.'
Quarter-page press advertisement in line.
Published: *Evening Standard*, 1 Jan. 1940, p. 12
Illustrated: *The Gentle Art of Advertising*, p. 73.

Burroughs Adding Machines Ltd

9. *Catching Runaway Pennies*, Burroughs Adding Machines Ltd., London, 1922.
275 × 215 mm, 8 pp.
An advertising leaflet with one line-drawing on the back page.
Note: There is evidence that Heath Robinson designed a series of blotters for Burroughs in 1922, but none have been seen.

Canadian Pacific

10. *The Story of Cocktails* as pictured by W. Heath Robinson and described by Anthony Armstrong. Reprinted from *The Strand Magazine*. Canadian Pacific, London, 1932.
186 × 244 mm, 16 pp.
Wrappers printed in black and orange.
Ten half-page illustrations and seven circular vignettes in orange and black half-tone, with a photograph of Heath Robinson painting one of them not reproduced in *The Strand Magazine*.

11. *Cocktail Mixing* shaken up by W. Heath Robinson. Canadian Pacific, London, nd (1938).
145 × 141 mm, 12 pp. (including wrappers).

180

Pictorial wrappers printed in orange and black.
Four full-page, five half-page and six circular vignette illustrations in orange and black half-tone.

City Dairy Co Ltd
12. *We Testify of That We Do Know*, City Dairy Co. Ltd, Toronto, Canada, nd (1903).
172 × 123 mm, 16 pp.
Brown wrappers with a pictorial design by WHR printed in black, red, blue and white.

Clarkhills Automatic Water Heaters Ltd
13. Half-tone picture for press advertisements.
Illustrated: *Commercial Art*, Mar. 1927, vol. 2, p. 115.

Connolly Bros (Curriers) Ltd
14. *Nothing Like Leather* by W. Heath Robinson, Connolly Bros (Curriers) Ltd, London, nd (1920).
217 × 139 mm, 12 pp.
Cream card covers decorated with silhouettes.
Six full-page and three smaller line-drawings.
Illustrated: *Art in Advertising* by P.V. Bradshaw, p. 329.

15. *Light on Leather* shed by W. Heath Robinson, Connolly Bros (Curriers) Ltd, London, nd (1922).
217 × 139 mm, 24 pp.
Cream card covers with pictorial design in red and black.
Six full-page and 17 smaller illustrations.
Illustrated: *Art in Advertising* by P.V. Bradshaw, p. 329.

16. *Tough Testimonials*, Connolly Bros (Curriers), London, nd (1924).
217 × 139 mm, 32 pp.
Cream card covers with a design by H.M. Bateman in red and black.
Numerous illustrations by H.M. Bateman, Rene Bull, F. Heubner, A. Leete, W. Heath Robinson,

H. Rountree, J. Routier, W. Sluiter, L. Tayler and A. Watts of which four line-drawings are by W. Heath Robinson.

17. *Nothing Takes the Place of Leather* by W. Heath Robinson, Connolly Bros (Curriers) Ltd, London, nd (1925).
139 × 217 mm, 20 pp.
Cream card covers with a pictorial design in red and black. Six full-page and 17 smaller line-drawings.

18. *Leather Breeding on the Wandle* described by W. Heath Robinson, Connolly Bros (Curriers) Ltd, nd (1927).
139 × 217 mm, 20 pp.
Cream card covers with a pictorial design in brown and black.
Six full-page and 14 smaller line-drawings.

19. *Cattle Culture at Connolly's Leather College on the Wandle*, described by W. Heath Robinson, Connolly Bros (Curriers) Ltd, London, nd (1930).
139 × 217 mm, 20 pp.
Cream card covers with a pictorial design in green and black.
Six full-page and 14 smaller line-drawings.

20. *Leather For Ever* by W. Heath Robinson, Connolly Bros (Curriers) Ltd, London, nd (1931).
217 × 139 mm, 20 pp.
Red and cream card covers with a pictorial design in black.
Six full-page and 14 smaller line-drawings.

21. *Heath Robinson on Leather* (collected edition), Connolly Bros. (Curriers) Ltd, London, nd (1932).
312 × 250 mm, 48 pp.
Brown leather-grained card covers with a pictorial design in black.
22 half-page, 82 smaller and six vignette line-drawings.
Note: All of the illustrations appeared in earlier Connolly booklets.

22. *Connolly Chronicles* retold by
W. Heath Robinson, Connolly Bros
(Curriers) Ltd, London, nd (1933).
272 × 194 mm, 20 pp.
Grey card covers printed in black and
white with a pictorial design.
Six full-page and 17 smaller
illustrations.

23. *Connolly-Land* by W. Heath
Robinson, Connolly Bros (Curriers)
Ltd, London, nd (1934).
258 × 134 mm, 14 pp. & fold-out
chart.
Grained beige card covers with a
pictorial design in black.
Five full-page and nine smaller line-
drawings, plus a triple page full-colour
fold-out plan.

24. *The Business Man's Encyclopedia
Connollyca*, compiled by W. Heath
Robinson, Connolly Bros (Curriers)
Ltd, London, nd (1935).
258 × 134 mm, 20 pp.
Cream and red grained-card cover
with a pictorial design in black.
36 half-page or smaller line-drawings.

25. *Connolly Customers* as imagined by
W. Heath Robinson, Connolly Bros
(Curriers) Ltd, London, nd (1936).
152 × 231 mm, 20 pp.
White card covers with a pictorial
design in blue and black.
Six full-page and 14 smaller line-
drawings.

26. *Heath Robinson on Leather* (collected
edition). Connolly Bros (Curriers)
Ltd, London, nd (1938).
312 × 250 mm, 48 pp.
Grey leather-grained card covers with
four silhouettes in black.
Six full-page, 22 half-page, 77 smaller
and six vignette line drawings.
Note: This is a revised version of the
1932 collection with six full-page
drawings from *Connolly Chronicles*
added.

27. *I Can't Improve on That, Mr
Connolly*. The story of Connolly
leather's first hundred years 1878–
1978. Connolly Bros (Curriers) Ltd,
London, 1978.
310 × 250 mm, 64 pp.
Brown leather-grained card covers
with a full-colour pictorial design.
Numerous photographs and a reprint
of *Heath Robinson on Leather*, 1932.

28. *Connolly Calendar, 1989*, Connolly
Bros (Curriers) Ltd, Wimbledon,
1988.
Limited edition of 1000 copies signed
by Oliver Robinson and Tim
Connolly.
485 × 380 mm, 14 spiral-bound leaves.
Pictorial card envelope printed in
cream, orange, grey and black.
13 line-drawings, one of which is
repeated on the cover, taken from
Light on Leather and *Leather for Ever*.
Printed on grained paper.

29. *Connolly Calendar, 1990*, Connolly
Bros (Curriers) Ltd, Wimbledon,
1989.
Limited edition of 1000 copies signed
by Oliver Robinson and Tim
Connolly.
380 × 478 mm, 14 spiral-bound leaves.
Pictorial card envelope printed in
black and grey.
Full-colour cover design of
'Connollyland', and 14 line-drawings
from *Leather Breeding on the Wandle*
and *Cattle Culture*.

30. *Connolly Calendar, 1991*, Connolly
Bros (Curriers) Ltd, Wimbledon,
1990.
Limited edition of 1000 copies signed
by Alan B. Robinson and Tim
Connolly.
477 × 382 mm, 14 spiral-bound leaves.
Pictorial card envelope printed in
cream, grey and black.
21 line-drawings reproduced from
Connolly Chronicles.

31. 'Connolly Bros Motor Hides'.
Full-page press advertisement in line
featuring the four silhouettes from the
cover of *Nothing Like Leather*.
Published: *The Home Made Car*,
Duckworth, nd (1921), p. 15.

Continental Tyre Company
32. Continental Tyre Co., Germany.
Two (or more?) full-page half-tone
cartoons in red and black featuring
Continental Ballon tyres.
Published in *Echo-Continental*, the
company house magazine in Germany,
nd (*c.* 1927).

William Cook & Co Ltd
33. Prospectus of William Cook & Co Ltd,
Sheffield, nd.
Size and format unknown.
Binding unknown.
Six full-page, half-tone illustrations.
Illustrated: *The Gentle Art of
Advertising*, pages 52–7.

Co-operative–Permanent Building Society
34. 'A Good Resolution.'
Quarter-page press advertisement in
line for Co-operative–Permanent
Building Society, London.
Published: *Evening Standard*, 1 Jan.
1934, p. 16
Illustrated: *The Gentle Art of
Advertising*, p. 76.

Robert Cort & Sons Ltd
35. *This Coke Business*. Robert Cort &
Sons Ltd, Reading, nd (1922).
219 × 214 mm, ? pp.
Pictorial cover design by W. Heath
Robinson printed in brown and black,
no other illustrations.
Illustrated: *The Gentle Art of
Advertising*, p. 88.

Courtaulds Ltd
36. 'A New Year's Resolution – To Make
Certain that Your Shirts and Pyjamas
bear the Registered LUVISCA Tab.'
Quarter-page press advertisement in
line.

Published: *Evening Standard*, 1 Jan
1934, p. 16.
Illustrated: *The Gentle Art of
Advertising*, p. 75.

William Crawford & Sons Ltd
37. 'Mr Heath Robinson's Conception of a
Modern Biscuit Plant.'
Full-page coloured press
advertisement for William Crawford &
Sons Ltd.
Published: *Punch* (Almanac Number),
6 Nov 1933.

The 'Cropwell' Herd
38. [Calendar for 1923].
Line drawing for a calendar
advertising Cuthbert C. Smith's
'Cropwell' herd of middle-white pigs
in Nottinghamshire.

The Daimler Company Ltd
39. *The Daimler Way of Ensuring Quality
Control*, The Daimler Company Ltd,
Coventry, nd.
Size and format unknown.
Binding unknown.
Two or more line drawings.
Illustrated: *Commercial Art*, Jun.
1927, vol. 2, p. 257.

The Direct Supply Aerated Water Co. Ltd
40. 'A Seasonable Resolution – Make sure
of a direct supply of refreshing drinks
throughout the coming year.'
Quarter-page press advertisement in
line for the Direct Supply Aerated
Water Co. Ltd.
Published: *Evening Standard*, 1 Jan.
1934, p. 17.

A. Duckham & Co. Ltd
41. *Technical Talks*, A. Duckham & Co.
Ltd, London, nd.
215 × 138 mm, 32 pp.
Blue card covers.
Six full-page half-tone illustrations.

G & T. Earle (1925) Ltd
42. *The Wonders of Wilmington*, depicted
by W. Heath Robinson, G. & T. Earle
(1925) Ltd, Wilmington, Hull, nd
(1928).

270 × 403 mm, 12 pp.
Pictorial leather-grained boards printed in black.
Five full-page half-tone illustrations.

43. *Earle's Early Etchings*, G. & T. Earle Ltd, Hull, 1949.
175 × 267 mm, 12 pp.
Pictorial wrappers with a photograph of Hope Works and Quarry.
Five full-page half-tone illustrations.
Note: The illustrations are reprinted from *The Wonders of Wilmington*.

J.C. Eno Ltd
44. 'The Buoyancy of Good Health.'
Full-page half-tone press advertisement for Eno's fruit salts.
Published: *Get on With It*, nd (1920).

Ever-Ready Razor Products Ltd
45. 'A Good New Year's Resolution – Be EVER READY in an Emergency.'
Quarter-page press advertisement in line.
Published: *Evening Standard*, 1 Jan. 1934, p. 17.

Firth Brothers
46. A rough sketch for a press advertisement of pianos exists. It is not known whether a finished drawing was made or published.

Fletcher, Burrows & Co. Ltd
47. *The 'First' Colliery*, an almanac of four drawings by W. Heath Robinson, With the Compliments of Fletcher, Burrows & Co. Ltd, Atherton, Lancashire, 1922.
548 × 358 mm, 5 pp.
Five cream-card leaves joined with a green silk cord passing through brass-reinforced holes.
Four mounted half-tone plates and a cover drawing in line.
Note: The calendar is unusual in running from April 1922 to March 1923. The calendar was reissued by Lancashire Associated Collieries in 1938.

Thomas Foreman & Son
48. Calendar issued by Thomas Foreman & Son, Nottingham (Printers), nd.
Format unknown.
12 coloured plates.
Note: These pictures were re-issued as greetings cards by Camden Graphics in 1982.

General Electric Co. Ltd
49. 'Osram Valves a tonic to any set.'
Published: *Printer's Pie*, 1934, p. 8
Illustrated: Chris Beetles Ltd Exhibition Catalogue, March 1987.
Note: A second, similar drawing was made for GEC, but its publication has not yet been traced.

Goodall, Backhouse & Co.
50. Yorkshire Relish
Full-colour design for showcard and postcard, nd.
Listed: Stanley Gibbons Postcard Catalogue, 1981.

Luis Gordon & Sons Ltd
51. 'Impressions of a Well Known Sherry Works by W. Heath Robinson.'
Coloured display card for Domecq's Sherry.
Illustrated: *The Gentle Art of Advertising*, p. 77.

The Great Western Railway
52. *Railway Ribaldry*, being 96 pages of railway humour by W. Heath Robinson, The Great Western Railway, Paddington Station, London, 1935.
247 × 186 mm, 96 pp.
Pictorial card wrappers printed in green, yellow and black.
45 full-page drawings and 52 vignettes in line.
Note: a few copies were bound up in paper-covered boards, probably for presentation.

The Gre-solvent Company
53. *The Tale Of A Great Discovery*, The Gre-solvent Company, Leeds, nd (1929).

125 × 175 mm, 8 pp.
Printed throughout on coarse yellow-brown paper.
11 line-drawings, one of which is repeated on the front.

W.P. Hartley

54. A new method of manufacturing marmalade.
A page of six line-drawings advertising Hartley's Marmalade.
Published: *Printer's Pie*, 1925, p. v.
Illustrated: *Meals on Wheels*, Souvenir Press, 1989, p. 10.
Note: These drawings look as if they were originally intended for a booklet.

Hazelbourne Laundry

55. *As Others See Us*, Hazelbourne Laundry, Balham, London, nd.
Date and size unknown.
Four-sheet fold-out leaflet on cream paper.
Seven line-drawings.

Hercules Cycle Co.

56. 'A Perfect Picnic on the All Weather Tandem.'
A full colour press advertisement for Hercules bicycles.
Published: *Hercules Cycle Magazine*, nd (1935).

High Duty Alloys Ltd

57. 'The War in the Air' by W. Heath Robinson. A series of full-page half-tone press advertisements for High Duty Alloys Ltd, Slough:

No.1. BLIND FLYING is flying when you can't exactly see where you are going – this is how young pilots are trained to do it.
Published: *Flight*, 11 Sept. 1941, advt. p. viii.

No. 2. AERO CAMOUFLAGE, a wartime expedient to make a plane indistinguishable from its background.
Published: *The Aeroplane*, 12 Sept. 1941, advt. p. 15.

No. 3. TO BALE OUT is to leave the plane at a moment's notice when your services are required elsewhere.
Published: *Flight*, 13 Nov. 1941, advt. p. 27.

No. 4. THE CRATE an old-fashioned but useful type of machine not yet adapted to wartime requirements.
Published: *Flight*, 25 Dec. 1941, advt. p. vii.

No. 5. THE CEILING is the highest point in the stratosphere at which the crew can carry on, and this is how they know when they get there.
Published: *Flight*, 5 Feb. 1942, advt. p. 25.

No. 6. 1942 MODEL. A new type especially designed to confuse the enemy by firing in all directions at the same time.
Published: *Flight*, 19 Mar. 1942, advt. p. 23.

No. 7. PARACHUTE LANDING. This is the improved method providing every comfort for the parachutist.
Published: *Flight*, 30 Apr. 1942, facing p. 440. Repeated 30 July 1942.

No. 8. MANOEUVRABILITY is the power to turn round quickly and dodge the snags in the line of flight.
Published: *Flight*, 11 Jun. 1942, advt. p. 19.
Note: It is probable that all of these drawings were published in both *Flight* and *The Aeroplane*, with the exception of No. 2 which does not seem to have appeared in *Flight*.

Horrockses' Crewdson & Co. Ltd

58. *How It Is Done!* The manufacture of cotton fabrics according to Heath Robinson – the famous humorist, Horrockses' Crewdson & Co. Ltd, Manchester 1921.
260 × 210 mm, 120 pp.
16 pages frontmatter, 104 pages diary interleaved with blotting paper.
Brown Morocco-grained cloth with a

coloured pictorial onlay.
Three full-page half-tone illustrations.

Hovis Ltd

59. *An Unconventional History of Hovis.*
Pictured by W. Heath Robinson.
Recounted by S.C. Peacock. Hovis
Ltd, Macclesfield, nd (1926).
247 × 188 mm, 24 pp.
Blue wrappers titled in black and tied
at the spine with blue cord.
10 full-page half-tone illustrations.

60. 'W. Heath Robinson on Hovis'.
Full-page, full-colour press
advertisement for Hovis Ltd.
Published: *The Sketch*, Christmas
Number 1926, p. 1.
Punch (Almanac Number), 1 Nov.
1926.
Nash's Pall Mall Magazine, Jan. 1927,
back cover.

Inecto

61. Press advertisement for Inecto hair
restorer, 1925.

International Stores

62. 'Delicate Apparatus for Testing
Cylindo Aroma.'
Press advertisement in line for Cylindo
Tea.
Published: *Cambridge Daily News*,
8 Oct. 1936, p. 6, and 5 Nov. 1936,
p. 2.

63. 'Something Worth Having.'
Press advertisement in line for
International Stores cakes and
biscuits.
Published: *Cambridge Daily News*,
22 Oct. 1936, p. 4.

Kado Carbon Papers

64. Advertisement in line for Kado
Carbon Papers.
Seen in a guide book. No details
available.

Kensitas

65. 'Kind to All Throats, Whipsnade
1931.'
Press advertisement in line for

Kensitas cigarettes.
Note: It is not known whether this was
published, but a rough drawing for it
was sold at Sotheby's in October 1989.

T. Kerfoot & Co.

66. 'The Manufacture and Testing of
Mineral Spring Granules.'
Four-panel press advertisement in line
for T. Kerfoot & Co., Bardsley,
Lancs.
Published: Spring 1922 (?)

Lamson Paragon Supply Company

67. Numerous press advertisements,
mainly in line, for Lamson Paragon
Supply Company, 4 Queen St,
Cheapside, London, advertising paper
bags, check books, 'plic' books and
other related products.
Published: *The Grocer*, *The Draper's
Record* and other trade magazines
between April 1903 and 1909.

68. Press advertisements mainly in line for
Lamson Paragon Company,
advertising M. & M. Paragon
Typewriter ribbons and Paragon
carbon paper.
Published: *Stationery Trades Journal*,
Pitman's Phonetic Journal and other
trade magazines in 1904–5.

Allen Lane

69. 'Mr W. Heath Robinson's Idea of a
Busy Afternoon in a Publisher's
Office.'
Christmas card, nd (*c*. 1933)
Illustrated: *The Private Library*,
vol. 7, no. 3, Autumn 1984, p. 132.
The Gentle Art of Advertising,
endpapers, (modified).

Lever Bros Ltd

70. 'Heath Robinson's Idea of Comfort.'
Published: *The Humorist*, 10 May
1924, p. 388
Illustrated: *Commercial Art*, Jun.
1927, vol. 2, p. 256
Note: This drawing was also included
in a portfolio of 12 drawings by

different artists advertising Comfort soap.

R.J. Lea Ltd

71. 'The Twelve Virtues of Chairman,' R.J. Lea Ltd, Manchester, 1915–16. A series of 12 full-page half-tone press advertisements for Chairman tobacco:

No. 1. 'Attractive Aroma.'
Published: *Punch* 14 Jul. 1915, p. v. *London Opinion*, 25 Sep. 1915, vol. 46, p. 466.

No. 2. 'A Solace to the Very End.'
Published: *Punch*, 11 Aug. 1915, p. vii.

No. 3. 'Entire Absence of Burning Sensation.'
Published: *Punch*, 8 Sep. 1915, p. vii. *London Opinion*, 16 Oct. 1915, vol. 47, p. 101.

No. 4. 'Fragrance Which All Enjoy.'
Published: *Punch*, 20 Oct. 1915, p. ix. *London Opinion*, 6 Nov. 1915, vol. 47, p. 245.

No. 5. 'Its Soothing Properties.'
Published: *Punch*, 10 Nov. 1915, p. ix. *London Opinion*, 27 Nov. 1915, vol. 47, p. 385.

No. 6. 'Promotes Geniality.'
Published: *Punch*, 8 Dec. 1915, p. ix. *London Opinion*, 8 Jan. 1916, vol. 48, p. 61.

No. 7. 'It Steadies the Nerves.'
Published: *Punch*, 12 Jan. 1916, p. ix. *London Opinion*, 29 Jan. 1916. vol. 48, p. 184.

No. 8. 'Its Taking Qualities.'
Published: *Punch*, 9 Feb. 1916, p. ix. *London Opinion*, 19 Feb. 1916. vol. 48, p. 300.

No. 9. 'Banishes Discomfort and Brings Content.'
Published: *Punch*, 8 Mar. 1916, p. ix. *London Opinion*, 11 Mar. 1916, vol. 48, p. 413.

No. 10. 'It Suits Most Palates.'
Published: *Punch*, 12 Apr. 1916, p. ix.

No. 11. 'It Promotes Mark Tapleyism.'
Published: *Punch*, 10 May 1916, p. ix.

No. 12. 'It is an Economy'
Published: *Punch*, 14 Jun. 1916, p. ix.

72. 'A Chairman Calamity.'
Full-page half-tone press advertisement for Chairman Tobacco. Published: *London Opinion* (Christmas Extra), 1915, p. 68. *Punch* (Almanac November), 1915 (pages unnumbered).

Limmer & Trinidad Lake Asphalt Co. Ltd

73. Full-colour drawing for use at a trade exhibition, Nov. 1921. 2000 prints of the picture were made for publicity purposes.

MacDonald, Greenlees & Williams (Distillers) Ltd

74. Sandy MacDonald's Scotch Whisky. Full-page, full-colour press advertisement Published: *The Sketch* (Christmas Number), 1922, p. 36.

J. Mackintosh & Sons Ltd

75. 'W. Heath Robinson's Impression of Toffee Town.' Full-page press advertisement in line for J. Mackintosh & Sons Ltd, Nottingham, advertising Toffee de Luxe. Published: *Daily Mail*, 1 Oct. 1921, front page. *The Sphere*, 22 Oct. 1921, p. viii. *The Passing Show*, 5 Nov. 1921.

76. 'Mackintosh's Toffee de Luxe is reduced to 8d per quarter – Heath Robinson's idea of how the news will be announced.' Press advertisement in line. Published: *Daily Mail*, 1 Dec. 1921, p. 14.

77. 'Mackintosh's call in the aid of Mr W. Heath Robinson to help Santa Claus

deliver Toffee de Luxe on Christmas
Eve.'
Full-page press advertisement in line.
Published: *Daily Mail*, 23 Dec. 1922,
front page.

Mazda

78. [Mazda light bulbs.]
Design for a showcard in 1921.

Meccano Ltd

79. 'Meccanotes.'
Double-page advertisement for
Meccano Ltd
One full-page half-tone illustration
and three small line drawings.
Published: *Get on With It*, 1920, pp.
50–1.

Moss Bros & Co Ltd

80. *Behind the Scenes at Moss Bros with
Heath Robinson*, Moss Bros & Co.
Ltd, Covent Garden, nd (1936).
218 × 295 mm, 16 pp.
Pictorial card covers printed in orange
and black.
15 full-page half-tone illustrations.
Illustrated: *The Gentle Art of
Advertising*, pp. 32–45.

Nabisco

81. 'How they cope with the New Year's
demand for Shredded Wheat.'
Quarter-page press advertisement in
line.
Published: *Evening Standard*, 1 Jan.
1940, p. 13.
Illustrated: *The Gentle Art of
Advertising*, p. 74.

Newton, Chambers & Co Ltd

82. *Thorncliffe Visited* by W. Heath
Robinson, Newton, Chambers & Co.
Ltd, Thorncliffe, Nr Sheffield, nd.
205 × 137 mm, 16 pp.
Pictorial card wrappers.
Seven full-page and two smaller
drawings in line.

83. *How Izal is Made*. Solid facts made
light by W. Heath Robinson, Newton,
Chambers & Co. Ltd, nd.
Size unknown, 16 pp.

Note: This is possibly a variant of
Thorncliffe Visited, using the same
drawings.

84. *Izal Kills Germs*. 10 postcards by
W. Heath Robinson, Newton,
Chambers & Co. Ltd, nd.
A set of 10 postcards, illustrated in
line, in a brown pictorial envelope.
Note: Four of the cards appear to have
been drawn in the early 1920s whilst
the other six are in a later 1930s style.
The envelope design was used on the
cover of *Thorncliffe Visited*.

The Nithsdale Silver Fox Ranch

85. *The Silver Fox Argosy*, The Nithsdale
Silver Fox Ranch, Thornhill,
Dumfries, 1934.
320 × 230 mm, [72 pp.].
Art vellum boards titled in black.
Numerous illustrations of which one
full-page and one smaller line-drawing
are by WHR.

Nugget

86. 'Resolve to put your best foot forward
– use Nugget boot polish and step
brightly through 1934.'
Quarter-page press advertisement in
line.
Published: *Evening Standard*, 1 Jan.
1934, p. 16.

87. 'Demonstrating the degree of
distinction to be acquired by all users
of Nugget.'
Quarter-page press advertisement in
line.
Published: *Evening Standard*, 1 Jan.
1937, p. 23.

88. 'Use Nugget boot polish and brighten
your outlook on life.'
Quarter-page press advertisement in
line.
Published: *Evening Standard*, 2 Jan.
1939, p. 17.

89. 'Begin the New Year well by joining
the long chain of users of Nugget boot
polish.'

Quarter-page press advertisement in line.
Published: *Evening Standard*, 1 Jan. 1940, p. 12.
Illustrated: *The Gentle Art of Advertising*, p. 72.

Oxo Ltd

90. Oxo press advertisement and/or showcard, 1922.
There are surviving letters to WHR from Oxo discussing these items, but no published examples have been seen. One drawing featured a billiard room with two white balls and the rest forming the word OXO. Another was called 'The Oxo Break'.

A. & F. Pears Ltd

91. 'The Unruffled Air.'
Double-page, half-tone illustration advertising Pears' Solid Brilliantine.
Published: *Get on With It*, 1920, pp. 28–9.

Peek Frean

92. 'The Heath Robinson Golf Course – Packed with Peek Frean's Biscuits.'
Full-colour design, possibly for a biscuit tin, nd.
Illustrated: Chris Beetles Ltd Exhibition Catalogue, Mar. 1984.

Philips Glowlamp Works Ltd

93. *The Wireless Adventures of Mr Pimple*, with compliments of Philips Glowlamp Works Ltd, 1924.
250 × 165 mm, 16 pp.
Cream card wrappers with a pictorial design in line.
Six full-page line-drawings and six vignettes.
Note: This booklet was also published with the text written in Dutch.

The Port of Manchester Warehouses Ltd

94. *Then and Now* illustrated by W Heath Robinson, The Port of Manchester Warehouses Ltd, Trafford Park, Manchester, 1921.
283 × 219 mm, 48 pp.
Brown paper wrappers with a pictorial

design in black and yellow.
Six full-page half-tone illustrations and 16 smaller line-drawings.
Illustrated: *The Gentle Art of Advertising*, pp. 46–51.

Hector Powe

95. 'The Evolution of a Pair of Trousers.'
A full-page press advertisement in line for Hector Powe, Tailors, London.
Published: *Pow-Wow*, the house magazine for Hector Powe *c*. 1924.
Reference: *Art in Advertising* by P.V. Bradshaw, 1925, p. 158.

The Practical Etching Service Ltd

96. *The Gentle Art of Reproducing*, W. Heath Robinson, Comments by A.P. Garland. The Practical Etching Service Ltd, London, nd (1931).
285 × 215 mm, 28 pp + fold-out plate.
Pictorial card wrappers printed in buff, green and black.
One full-colour double-page illustration and 11 full-page half-tone illustrations.
Illustrated: *The Gentle Art of Advertising*, pp. 58–69.

Procter Bros (Wireworks) Ltd

97. 'The Toasted Cheese Method – This isn't the only way to catch mice, Try the Little Nipper.'
Full-colour design for showcard and postcard, nd.
Reproduced as a greetings card by Athena International, London, *c*. 1976.

Prudential Assurance Co. Ltd

98. 'A simple device for showing at a glance the position of your insurance – with gramophone adjustment for use at the New Year.'
Quarter-page press advertisement in line.
Published: *Evening Standard*, 1 Jan. 1934, p. 17.

Stiff & Co.

99. [The Manufacture of Remy's Macaroni.]

Press advertisement in line for Stiff &
Co, Starch Manufacturers.
Published: In Belgium, 1922.
Note: Heath Robinson also designed a
poster advertising Remy's Starch some
years earlier.

Rhodian Cigarettes

100. 'The manufacture of Rhodian
cigarettes.'
Quarter-page press advertisement in
line.
Published: *Evening Standard*, 1 Jan.
1937, p. 23.

101. 'Testing the aroma of Rhodian
cigarettes with the new natural
flavour.'
Quarter-page press advertisement in
line.
Published: *Evening Standard*, 2 Jan.
1939, p. 17.

Rogers Peet Company

102. *Some Trade Secrets Revealed*, by
Rogers Peet Company, New York,
nd (1927).
Size and number of pages unknown.
Binding style unknown.
Six full-page drawings in line.
Illustrated: *Printed Salesmanship*,
Cambridge, Mass., Jun. 1927,
pp. 346–7.
The Gentle Art of Advertising,
pp. 26–31.

Ruston-Bucyrus Ltd

103. *The Gentle Art of Excavating*, W.
Heath Robinson, issued with the
compliments of Ruston-Bucyrus Ltd,
Lincoln, nd. (*c*. 1938).
272 × 222 mm, 12 pp.
Light brown card wrappers, printed
in dark brown.
Six full-page half-tone illustrations
and 10 smaller line drawings.
Illustrated: *The Gentle Art of
Advertising*, pp. 11–19.
Chris Beetles Ltd Exhibition
Catalogue, 1987, p. 127.

Schuck, Maclean & Co. Ltd

104. *Life Without Printing Ink*, Schuck,
Maclean & Co. Ltd, nd.
Size unknown.
Wrappers secured by silk bow at top
corner.
Six full-colour plates of which one is
by WHR.
Illustrated: The WHR plate
reproduced in monochrome in
Commercial Art, Jun. 1927, vol. 2,
p. 258.

Smith's Sectric Clocks

105. 'A Good Resolution for the New
Year – Install in every room Smith's
Synchronous Electric Clocks.'
Press advertisement in line.
Published: *Evening Standard*, 1 Jan.
1934, p. 17.

106. 'The sealing-wax test of the correct
synchronisation of Smith electric
clocks at noon.'
Press advertisement in line.
Published: *Evening Standard*, 1 Jan.
1937, p. 23.

107. 'The sun test for sectric clocks.'
Press advertisement in line for
Smith's electric clocks.
Published: *Evening Standard*, 2 Jan.
1939, p. 17.

108. 'Plug in at Greenwich – Smith's
Sectric Clocks enable you to start all
the days of the New Year on time.'
Press advertisement in line.
Published: *Evening Standard*, 1 Jan.
1940, p. 12.
Illustrated: *The Gentle Art of
Advertising*, p. 71.

Standard Fireworks

109. 'How Standard Fireworks are made'
and 'Some Uses for Standard
Fireworks'.
Two drawings for press
advertisements and/or posters, nd.
Exhibited: Hornsey Library, 13 Jan.
1973.

Douglas Stuart

110. 'When You're Putting Your Shirt on a Horse – Tell "Duggie" all about it.'
Press advertisement in line for Douglas Stuart, bookmaker, Stuart House, Shaftesbury Avenue, London.
Published: *Illustrated Sporting and Dramatic News*, 31 Jan. 1936 and 2 Apr. 1937, back covers.

111. 'There's Absolutely No Limit to What You Can Put On a Horse If You – Tell "Duggie" all about it.'
Press advertisement in line.
Published: *Illustrated Sporting and Dramatic News*, 7 Feb. 1936 and 28 Feb. 1936, back covers.

112. 'When Getting a Tip Straight from the Horse's Mouth – Tell "Duggie" all about it.'
Press advertisement in line.
Published: *Illustrated Sporting and Dramatic News*, 14 Feb. 1936, back cover.

113. 'When Backing a Horse in Your Own Home – Tell "Duggie" all about it.'
Press advertisement in line.
Published: *Illustrated Sporting and Dramatic News*, 21 Feb. 1936, 4 Sep. 1936 and 5 Feb. 1937, back covers.

114. 'If You're Picking a Horse Blindly – Back it with your eyes open.'
Press advertisement in line.
Published: *Illustrated Sporting and Dramatic News*, 6 Mar. 1936, back cover.

115. 'If You Must Have Something On – Tell "Duggie" all about it.'
Press advertisement in line.
Published: *Illustrated Sporting and Dramatic News*, 10 Apr. 1936, back cover.
Illustrated London News, 27 Jun. 1936, back cover.

116. 'If You Want to be in On a Good Double Event – Tell "Duggie" all about it.'
Press advertisement in line.
Published: *Illustrated Sporting and Dramatic News*, 1 May 1936, back cover.

117. 'If You are About to Put a "Monkey" On a Horse – Tell "Duggie" all about it.'
Press advertisement in line.
Published: *Illustrated Sporting and Dramatic News*, 26 Feb. 1937, back cover.

Thomas Tapling Ltd

118. 'The Gentle Art of Making Feather Beds' and 'The Gentle Art of Making Down Quilts'.
Two drawings for press advertisements/showcards, nd.
Illustrated: The latter illustrated in *The Gentle Art of Advertising*, p. 87.

Thomas & Green Ltd

119. *The Art of Papermaking* as Explained by W. Heath Robinson, a calendar for 1922. Thomas & Green Ltd, Wooburn Green, Bucks, 1921.
A single board covered in handmade paper.
530 × 390 mm
Nine small drawings in full colour plus mounted tear-off date tablet.
Produced by G. Heath Robinson & J. Birch Ltd, 17 & 18 Took's Court, London EC4.
Also published as a press advertisement in *The British Printer*, vol. 34, no. 203, Jan.–Feb. 1922, facing p. 228.

Turnbull

120. Drawings for *Turnbull's Quarterly*, also published as prints.
Turnbull [cleaners and dyers], nd.

Vickerys Ltd

121. 'Interesting Experiments in the Research Department of Vickerys Ltd, Paper Mill Specialities' and 'Stages in the Evolution of Vickery Doctoring'.
Two drawings for press

advertisements and/or wall cards for Vickerys Ltd, Lambeth Palace Road, London SE1.
Illustrated: *The Gentle Art of Advertising*, pp. 84–5.

Wagon Repair Company

122. *At Your Service*, a list of agents of the Wagon Repair Company.
180 × 120 mm, 103 pp.
Blue cloth blocked in black.
Illustrated endpapers in red and black, the front by WHR, the back by Will Owen.

Johnnie Walker

123. Johnnie Walker Whisky.
Six full-page half-tone illustrations, possibly for a calendar, nd [1915].
Illustrated: *The Gentle Art of Advertising*, pp. 20–5.
Reprinted: *The Johnnie Walker Heath Robinson Prints*, 1987. Six full-scale reproductions printed in sepia on cream paper, bound calendar-style.

Wellington & Ward Ltd

124. *The Light Side of Photography* illustrated by W. Heath Robinson, Wellington & Ward Ltd, Elstree, Herts, nd (*c*. 1925).
250 × 185 mm, 16 pp.
Pictorial wrappers.
12 full-page half-tone illustrations and a cover design in line.
Note: These drawings were also used for press advertisements in *The New Photographer* in 1925.

Wright, Layman & Umney Ltd

125. 'Some new machinery for putting the final touches to toilet soap.'
Quarter-page press advertisement in line for Wright's Coal Tar Soap.
Published: *Evening Standard*, 1 Jan. 1934, p. 16.
Illustrated: *The Gentle Art of Advertising*, p. 70.

126. 'Coping with the extra demand in Coronation Year. The wrapping and packing department.'
Quarter-page press advertisement in line for Wright's Coal Tar Soap.
Published: *Evening Standard*, 1 Jan. 1937, p. 23

127. 'The latest stages in the development of a perfect toilet soap.'
Quarter-page press advertisement in line for Wright's Coal Tar Soap.
Published: *Evening Standard*, 2 Jan. 1939, p. 17.

128. 'Wright's Coal Tar Soap – the soap for everybody in the New Year.'
Quarter-page press advertisement in line for Wright's Coal Tar Soap.
Published: *Evening Standard*, 1 Jan. 1940, p. 12.

Youngman Ladders

129. 'Take No Chances –', Youngman Ladders, nd.
166 × 101 mm, 4-page leaflet.
Full-page line-drawing on the front, printed in brown on pink paper.

Zerkall Bütten

130. *Zerkall Bütten Auf Der Maschine Geschopft*, Zerkall Bütten, nd.
150 × 115 mm, 3 panels, folded zig-zag style, on hand-made paper.
Three full-page line-drawings printed in grey.